Kyarf

Environmentalism

Lauri S. Friedman, *Book Editor*

GREENHAVEN PRESS
A part of Gale, Cengage Learning

Detroit • New York • San Francisco • New Haven, Conn • Waterville, Maine • London

Elizabeth Des Chenes, *Managing Editor*

For more information, contact:
Greenhaven Press
27500 Drake Rd.
Farmington Hills, MI 48331-3535
Or you can visit our Internet site at gale.cengage.com

Articles in Greenhaven Press anthologies are often edited for length to meet page requirements. In addition, original titles of these works are changed to clearly present the main thesis and to explicitly indicate the author's opinion. Every effort is made to ensure that Greenhaven Press accurately reflects the original intent of the authors. Every effort has been made to trace the owners of copyrighted material.

LIBRARY OF CONGRESS CATALOGING-IN-PUBLICATION DATA

Environmentalism / Lauri S. Friedman, book editor.
p. cm. -- (Introducing issues with opposing viewpoints)
Includes bibliographical references and index.
ISBN 978-0-7377-5677-7 (hardcover)
1. Environmentalism--Juvenile literature. I. Friedman, Lauri S.
GE195.5.E595 2012
333.72--dc23

2011030167

Printed in the United States of America
1 2 3 4 5 6 7 15 14 13 12 11

Contents

Foreword

Indulging in a wide spectrum of ideas, beliefs, and perspectives is a critical cornerstone of democracy. After all, it is often debates over differences of opinion, such as whether to legalize abortion, how to treat prisoners, or when to enact the death penalty, that shape our society and drive it forward. Such diversity of thought is frequently regarded as the hallmark of a healthy and civilized culture. As the Reverend Clifford Schutjer of the First Congregational Church in Mansfield, Ohio, declared in a 2001 sermon, "Surrounding oneself with only like-minded people, restricting what we listen to or read only to what we find agreeable is irresponsible. Refusing to entertain doubts once we make up our minds is a subtle but deadly form of arrogance." With this advice in mind, Introducing Issues with Opposing Viewpoints books aim to open readers' minds to the critically divergent views that comprise our world's most important debates.

Introducing Issues with Opposing Viewpoints simplifies for students the enormous and often overwhelming mass of material now available via print and electronic media. Collected in every volume is an array of opinions that captures the essence of a particular controversy or topic. Introducing Issues with Opposing Viewpoints books embody the spirit of nineteenth-century journalist Charles A. Dana's axiom: "Fight for your opinions, but do not believe that they contain the whole truth, or the only truth." Absorbing such contrasting opinions teaches students to analyze the strength of an argument and compare it to its opposition. From this process readers can inform and strengthen their own opinions, or be exposed to new information that will change their minds. Introducing Issues with Opposing Viewpoints is a mosaic of different voices. The authors are statesmen, pundits, academics, journalists, corporations, and ordinary people who have felt compelled to share their experiences and ideas in a public forum. Their words have been collected from newspapers, journals, books, speeches, interviews, and the Internet, the fastest growing body of opinionated material in the world.

Introducing Issues with Opposing Viewpoints shares many of the well-known features of its critically acclaimed parent series, Opposing Viewpoints. The articles are presented in a pro/con format, allowing readers to absorb divergent perspectives side by side. Active reading questions preface each viewpoint, requiring the student to approach the material thoughtfully and carefully. Useful charts, graphs, and cartoons supplement each article. A thorough introduction provides readers with crucial background on an issue. An annotated bibliography points the reader toward articles, books, and websites that contain additional information on the topic. An appendix of organizations to contact contains a wide variety of charities, nonprofit organizations, political groups, and private enterprises that each hold a position on the issue at hand. Finally, a comprehensive index allows readers to locate content quickly and efficiently.

Introducing Issues with Opposing Viewpoints is also significantly different from Opposing Viewpoints. As the series title implies, its presentation will help introduce students to the concept of opposing viewpoints and learn to use this material to aid in critical writing and debate. The series' four-color, accessible format makes the books attractive and inviting to readers of all levels. In addition, each viewpoint has been carefully edited to maximize a reader's understanding of the content. Short but thorough viewpoints capture the essence of an argument. A substantial, thought-provoking essay question placed at the end of each viewpoint asks the student to further investigate the issues raised in the viewpoint, compare and contrast two authors' arguments, or consider how one might go about forming an opinion on the topic at hand. Each viewpoint contains sidebars that include at-a-glance information and handy statistics. A Facts About section located in the back of the book further supplies students with relevant facts and figures.

Following in the tradition of the Opposing Viewpoints series, Greenhaven Press continues to provide readers with invaluable exposure to the controversial issues that shape our world. As John Stuart Mill once wrote: "The only way in which a human being can make some approach to knowing the whole of a subject is by hearing what can be said about it by persons of every variety of opinion and studying all modes in which it can be looked at by every character of mind. No wise man ever acquired his wisdom in any mode but this." It is to this principle that Introducing Issues with Opposing Viewpoints books are dedicated.

Introduction

Environmentalists are often accused of putting the interests of animals, plants, and ecosystems over the interests of human beings or even of sacrificing human needs and interests for the sake of the environment. Yet environmentalists believe that protecting the planet is ultimately in the interest of all humans, who require clean air, water, and land to thrive. This tension—of whether environmentalism serves or is at odds with human beings' best interests—is at the heart of many of the debates about what to do about global warming, habitat loss, endangered species, development, pollution, and other environmental issues.

From the perspective of antienvironmentalists, environmentalists seek to curb human development when they pursue policies and actions that limit, financially penalize, or otherwise inconvenience humans. For example, environmentalists typically support or seek taxes on substances that will harm the environment, in the hopes it will discourage their use. They also pursue policies that limit the kinds or amounts of pollutants that can be emitted, which in turn can make products more expensive and can drive some companies to cut jobs. Václav Klaus, president of the Czech Republic, has gone so far as to call environmentalism an "anti-human ideology" because of the way it proposes to limit human production, growth, and even enjoyment. "[Environmentalism is] always based on the idea that the starting point of our thinking should be the Earth, the planet or nature, not man or mankind," says Klaus. "Many environmentalists want to save the planet, not mankind."[1]

Environmentalists would claim that nothing could be further from the truth. In their eyes, they are passionate about the needs, rights, and future development and prospects of human beings. They say their interest in saving the planet stems precisely from their belief that without a healthy environment, humans *have* no future. In other words, the interests of the environment and of humans are inextricably linked. "All humanists are intrinsically environmentalists because they know that [no one can save them] once total damage is done to the natural resources on which they live and flourish," writes Rekha Saraswat, managing editor of the Indian publication the *Radical Humanist.*

"Therefore, for the sake of its own existence, Humanism can never be averse to Environmentalism."[2]

Most Americans wrestle with these two positions. Most want to do what is right for the environment, yet they also want to enjoy their lives with few interruptions or inconveniences. Polls have repeatedly shown that although most Americans claim to care about environmental issues, few are willing to make meaningful sacrifices in the environment's behalf. An extensive ABC News/ *Washington Post*/Stanford University poll taken in 2007, for example, revealed Americans' ambivalence in this area. A whopping 94 percent of Americans said they were either somewhat or very willing to change their behavior to help the environment, and 85 percent said they would feel this way even if the changes required some personal inconvenience.

Yet when pollsters probed them on exactly what kinds of measures they would accept, many fewer Americans were willing to make or accept such changes. In general, the majority of Americans said they were opposed to increasing taxes on electricity so people use less of it (79 percent opposed) and increasing taxes on gasoline so people either drive less or buy cars that use less gas (67 percent opposed). Majorities of Americans also thought manufacturers should not be required to build cars that use less gasoline; build air conditioners, refrigerators, and other appliances that use less electricity; or build new homes and offices that use less energy. The only proposal that the majority (62 percent) of Americans thought should be required was to make power plants lower the amount of greenhouse gases they are allowed to release into the air—something, it should be noted, that does not require a direct sacrifice on the part of individuals.

Indeed, Americans are notorious for supporting feel-good, easy, and inexpensive environmental measures that require little sacrifice or change, such as using shopping bags made of recyclable materials rather than plastic (a measure that 82 percent said they would support). They are decidedly more hesitant, however, to adopt more serious measures that require more energy, money, and time, such as driving less or carpooling (which a 2008 Gallup poll found that only 17 percent of Americans were willing to do), or driving a more fuel-efficient vehicle (which just 9 percent said they were willing to do). Yet it is these more intensive actions that are likely to have a measurable impact on the planet's environmental health, while smaller, superficial ones will not. As investigative journalist Tina Dupuy puts it, "Contrary to the sign at the grocery store, it's pretty safe to say you will not be able to save the Earth by purchasing a reusable bag."[3]

How far Americans are willing to change their daily lifestyles to support environmentalism is likely to ebb and flow in the coming years. Whether environmentalism is necessary, helpful, or critical, and whether environmentalists are alarmists, terrorists, or visionaries, are some of the many topics debated in *Introducing Issues with Opposing Viewpoints: Environmentalism.* The authors put forth arguments about whether threats to the environment are real, whether environmentalism threatens or boosts economic growth and job creations, and what the state of the environmental movement is today. Guided reading questions and challenging essay prompts encourage readers to develop their own opinions on this twenty-first-century topic.

Notes

1. Václav Klaus, "An Anti-Human Ideology," *Financial Post,* October 20, 2010. http://opinion.financialpost.com/2010/10/20/vaclav-klaus-an-anti-human-ideology.
2. Rekha Saraswat, "Is Humanism Averse to Environmentalism?," *Radical Humanist,* May 31, 2010. www.theradicalhumanist.com/index.php?option=com_radical&controller=editorials&cid=19&Itemid=67.
3. Tina Dupuy, "Stop Trying to 'Save the Planet,'" *Huffington Post,* March 8, 2010. www.huffingtonpost.com/tina-dupuy/stop-trying-to-save-the-p_b_490355.html.

Chapter 1

Is Environmentalism Necessary?

Whether the planet needs protecting is a topic of ongoing debate.

Environmentalism Is Necessary

Andrew Simms

"In just 100 months' time . . . we could reach a tipping point for the beginnings of runaway climate change."

In the following viewpoint Andrew Simms warns that the world is on the brink of serious, irreversible environmental disaster. He explains that an atmospheric buildup of carbon dioxide (CO_2) is threatening to raise the earth's surface temperature by two degrees Celsius. Although this may not sound like a significant amount, Simms warns that such a temperature increase would be enough to trigger catastrophic environmental changes, such as rising seas, massive ice loss, and severe weather. Such changes would be disastrous for all forms of life, he asserts. Simms concludes that major environmental changes are needed if the planet is to be saved from catastrophic climate change.

Andrew Simms is policy director and head of the climate change program at the New Economics Foundation, a British think tank.

AS YOU READ, CONSIDER THE FOLLOWING QUESTIONS:

1. How many metric tons of carbon dioxide does Simms say have been released into the atmosphere over the last 250 years?
2. What does the author warn will be triggered by a temperature increase of 2.7 degrees Celsius?
3. What does the word "unburnable" mean in the context of the viewpoint?

Andrew Simms, "We Have Only 100 Months to Avoid Irreversible Environmental Disaster," *Guardian,* August 1, 2008.

If you shout "fire" in a crowded theatre, when there is none, you understand that you might be arrested for irresponsible behaviour and breach of the peace. But from today, I smell smoke, I see flames and I think it is time to shout. I don't want you to panic, but I do think it would be a good idea to form an orderly queue to leave the building.

Because in just 100 months' time, if we are lucky, and based on a quite conservative estimate, we could reach a tipping point for the beginnings of runaway climate change. That said, among people working on global warming, there are countless models, scenarios, and different iterations of all those models and scenarios. So, let us be clear from the outset about exactly what we mean.

A Critical Tipping Point

The concentration of carbon dioxide (CO_2) in the atmosphere today, the most prevalent greenhouse gas, is the highest it has been for the past 650,000 years. In the space of just 250 years, as a result of the coal-fired Industrial Revolution, and changes to land use such as the growth of cities and the felling of forests, we have released, cumulatively, more than 1,800bn tonnes [billion metric tons] of CO_2 into the atmosphere. Currently, approximately 1,000 tonnes of CO_2 are released into the Earth's atmosphere every second, due to human activity. Greenhouse gases trap incoming solar radiation, warming the atmosphere. When these gases accumulate beyond a certain level—often termed a "tipping point"—global warming will accelerate, potentially beyond control.

Faced with circumstances that clearly threaten human civilisation, scientists at least have the sense of humour to term what drives this process as "positive feedback". But if translated into an office workplace environment, it's the sort of "positive feedback" from a manager that would run along the lines of: "You're fired, you were rubbish anyway, you have no future, your home has been demolished and I've killed your dog."

In climate change, a number of feedback loops amplify warming through physical processes that are either triggered by the initial warming itself, or the increase in greenhouse gases. One example is the melting of ice sheets. The loss of ice cover reduces the ability of the Earth's

As a result of the coal-fired Industrial Revolution, 1,800 billion metric tons of CO_2 have been released into the atmosphere over the past 250 years.

surface to reflect heat and, by revealing darker surfaces, increases the amount of heat absorbed. Other dynamics include the decreasing ability of oceans to absorb CO_2 due to higher wind strengths linked to climate change. This has already been observed in the Southern Ocean and North Atlantic, increasing the amount of CO_2 in the atmosphere, and adding to climate change.

Because of such self-reinforcing positive feedbacks (which, because of the accidental humour of science, we must remind ourselves are, in fact, negative), once a critical greenhouse concentration threshold is passed, global warming will continue even if we stop releasing additional greenhouse gases into the atmosphere. If that happens, the Earth's climate will shift into another, more volatile state, with different ocean circulation, wind and rainfall patterns. The implications of which, according to a growing litany of research, are potentially catastrophic for life on Earth. Such a change in the state of the climate system is often referred to as irreversible climate change.

A Hundred Months Left

So, how exactly do we arrive at the ticking clock of 100 months? It's possible to estimate the length of time it will take to reach a tipping point. To do so you combine current greenhouse gas concentrations with the best estimates for the rates at which emissions are growing, the maximum concentration of greenhouse gases allowable to forestall potentially irreversible changes to the climate system, and the effect of those environmental feedbacks. We followed the latest data and trends for carbon dioxide, then made allowances for all human interferences that influence temperatures, both those with warming and cooling effects. We followed the judgments of the mainstream climate science community, represented by the Intergovernmental Panel on Climate Change (IPCC), on what it will take to retain a good chance of not crossing the critical threshold of the Earth's average surface temperature rising by 2C [two degrees Celsius] above pre-industrial levels. We were cautious

Fast Fact

According to a 2010 Committee Against Oil Exploration report, a single oil rig can, over its lifetime, dump more than ninety thousand metric tons of drilling fluid and metal cuttings into the ocean. It can also drill fifty to one hundred wells, each of which dumps twenty-five thousand pounds of toxic metals and potent carcinogens into the ocean and pollutes the air as much as seven thousand cars driving fifty miles a day.

in several ways, optimistic even, and perhaps too much so. A rise of 2C may mask big problems that begin at a lower level of warming. For example, collapse of the Greenland ice sheet is more than likely to be triggered by a local warming of 2.7C, which could correspond to a global mean temperature increase of 2C or less. The disintegration of the Greenland ice sheet could correspond to a sea-level rise of up to 7 metres.

In arriving at our timescale, we also used the lower end of threats in assessing the impact of vanishing ice cover and other carbon-cycle feedbacks. . . . But the result is worrying enough.

We found that, given all of the above, 100 months from today we will reach a concentration of greenhouse gases at which it is no longer "likely" that we will stay below the 2C temperature rise threshold. "Likely" in this context refers to the definition of risk used by the IPCC. But, even just before that point, there is still a one third chance of crossing the line.

We Must Act Now

Today is just another Friday in August. Drowsy and close. Office workers' minds are fixed on the weekend, clock-watching, waiting perhaps for a holiday if your finances have escaped the credit crunch and rising food and fuel prices. In the evening, trains will be littered with abandoned newspaper sports pages, all pretending interest in the football transfers. For once it seems justified to repeat [poet] TS Eliot's famous lines: "This is the way the world ends/Not with a bang but a whimper." But does it have to be this way? Must we curdle in our complacency and allow our cynicism about politicians to give them an easy ride as they fail to act in our, the national and the planet's best interest? There is now a different clock to watch than the one on the office wall. Contrary to being a counsel of despair, it tells us that everything we do from now [on] matters. And, possibly more so than at any other time in recent history. . . .

So what can our own government do to turn things around today? Over the next 100 months, they could launch a Green New Deal, taking inspiration from President [Franklin] Roosevelt's famous 100-day programme implementing his New Deal in the face of the dust bowls and depression. Last week [in July 2008], a group of finance, energy and environmental specialists produced just such a plan.

A Plan to Save the Planet

Addressed at the triple crunch of the credit crisis, high oil prices and global warming, the plan is to rein in reckless financial institutions and use a range of fiscal tools, new measures and reforms to the tax system, such as a windfall tax on oil companies. The resources raised can then be invested in a massive environmental transformation programme that could insulate the economy from recession, create countless new jobs and allow Britain to play its part in meeting the climate challenge.

Goodbye new airport runways, goodbye new coal-fired power stations. Next, as a precursor to enabling and building more sustainable systems for transport, energy, food and overhauling the nation's building stock, the government needs to brace itself to tackle the City [the area of London that is the seat of the UK financial services industry]. Currently, financial institutions are giving us the worst of all worlds. We have woken to find the foundations of our economy made up of unstable, exotic financial instruments. At the same time, and perversely, as awareness of climate change goes up, ever more money pours through the City into the oil companies. These companies list their fossil-fuel reserves as "proven" or "probable". A new category of "unburnable" [referring to the concept that fossil-fuel reserves should stay in the ground to avoid accelerating climate change] should be introduced, to fundamentally change the balance of power in the City. Instead of using vast sums of public money to bail out banks because they are considered "too big to fail", they should be reduced in size until they are small enough to fail without hurting anyone. It is only a climate system capable of supporting human civilisation that is too big to fail.

Oil companies made profits when oil was $10 a barrel. With the price now wobbling around $130, there is a huge amount of unearned profit waiting for a windfall tax. Money raised—in this way and through other changes in taxation, new priorities for pension funds and innovatory types of bonds—would go towards a long-overdue massive decarbonisation of our energy system. Decentralisation, renewables, efficiency, conservation and demand management will all play a part.

Effect of Global Warming on Species and Natural Habitats

Scientists say a temperature increase of just 2°C would have serious environmental consequences; an increase of 4°C would be catastrophic.

Temperature rise above pre-industrial levels (in degrees Celsius)	Effect
+3.7°C	Few ecosystems able to adapt
+3.4°C	Substantial loss of northern forests (China)
	Habitat of many migrating birds destroyed
+3.1°C	Disappearance of remaining coral reef systems
	Risk of extinction of Alpine species (Europe)
+2.9°C	21–36% of butterfly species become extinct (Australia)
	21–52% of all species face extinction
+2.8°C	Loss of 62% of summer Arctic ice, polar bears face extinction
+2.6°C	Probable extinction of 4–21% of plants (Europe)
+2.5°C	>2.5°C a major turning point: forests, soils and plants start to produce more CO_2 than they absorb
	Major destruction of Amazon rainforest
+2.3°C	Probable extinction of 24–59% of mammals, 28–40% of birds, 13–70% of butterflies and 21–45% of reptiles (South Africa)
	24% loss of freshwater fish habitat, 27% loss of salmon (N. America)
+2.2°C	15–37% of all species face extinction
	8–20% increase in forest fires (Mediterranean)
+2.1°C	41–51% loss of all endemic plant species (S. Africa, Namibia)
+1.9°C	47% of rainforest habitat lost with extinctions of up to 14% of reptiles, 18% of frogs, 10% of birds, 15% of mammals (Northern Australia)
+1.7°C	All coral reefs are bleached
+1.6°C	9–31% of all species face extinction
+1°C	Reduced krill (Arctic, Antarctic), possibly affecting Adelie penguin populations
+0.6°C	Increased coral bleaching (Caribbean, Indian Ocean, Great Barrier Reef)

Taken from: Intergovernmental Panel on Climate Change, 2009.

Next comes a rolling programme to overhaul the nation's heat-leaking building stock. This will have the benefit of massively cutting emissions and at the same time tackling the sore of fuel poverty by creating better insulated and designed homes. A transition from "one person, one car" on the roads, to a variety of clean reliable forms of public transport should be visible by the middle of our 100 months. Similarly, weaning agriculture off fossil-fuel dependency will be a phased process.

Real Leadership Is Needed

The end result will be real international leadership, removing the excuses of other nations not to act. But it will also leave the people of Britain more secure in terms of the food and energy supplies, and with a more resilient economy capable of weathering whatever economic and environmental shocks the world has to throw at us. Each of these challenges will draw on things that we already know how to do, but have missed the political will for.

So, there, I have said "Fire", and pointed to the nearest emergency exit. Now it is time for the government to lead, and do its best to make sure that neither a bang, nor a whimper ends the show.

EVALUATING THE AUTHOR'S ARGUMENTS:

As part of his argument that environmentalism is necessary, Andrew Simms suggests it is time to launch a Green New Deal. Explain what he means by this. Then, state how you think Meredith Turney, author of the following viewpoint, would respond to this plan. Finally, state with which author you agree. Quote from both authors in explaining your answer.

Environmentalism Is Not Necessary

Meredith Turney

"Americans have sacrificed their lives so that other nations could enjoy the very freedom the environmentalism tyranny seeks to steal."

Environmentalism is unnecessary and needlessly burdens the American people, argues Meredith Turney in the following viewpoint. She suggests that global warming proponents are much like Chicken Little, who frantically (and falsely) warned of impending doom. In Turney's opinion, the planet does not need saving, and environmental regulations geared to this end are wasteful, unfair, and unnecessary. Turney laments that the American people have been forced to change the kinds of cars they drive, the products they buy, and the way they use water. More useful, in her opinion, would be American innovations and inventions that solve current problems and inspire Americans to dream and grow. She concludes that environmental regulations cost money, kill jobs, and force the American people to make sacrifices that are both unfair and unnecessary.

Meredith Turney is communications director for Media and Public Affairs Strategy and the California communications director for Americans for Prosperity.

Meredith Turney, "America's Unnecessary Sacrifice for the Planet," Townhall.com, December 1, 2009. Reproduced by permission of the author.

AS YOU READ, CONSIDER THE FOLLOWING QUESTIONS:

1. What is Assembly Bill 32, and what effect does Turney say it had on California?
2. What does Turney say Americans have been scolded for, and why does she think this is inappropriate?
3. What, in the author's opinion, kills creativity?

As President [Barack] Obama heads to Copenhagen next week [in December 2009] to meet with world leaders at the United Nations Climate Change Summit, there will undoubtedly be countless calls for tighter restrictions on all the demonized activities that supposedly cause global warming. Burning up carbon-based fuel as they fly in on their private jets, wining and dining like the elite, attendees of the Summit will spend days pontificating on the dire state of the planet—caused by the evil, greedy men who aren't in attendance—and then push radical plans to curb any modern, productive ventures that they perceive as contributing to nebulous "climate change."

Global warming disciples will denounce America as the chief cause of climate change because of its consumer-driven, greedy, capitalist-based economy. The country that brought about the highest standards of living the world has ever known will be denounced as the greatest danger to the world's future. To assuage global elitists and offer penance for her sins against Mother Earth, America will be required to subscribe to a new (sub)standard of living.

Environmentalist Regulations Choke Economic Growth

What can Americans expect if President Obama agrees to drastic new global warming standards for the entire nation? California offers a cautionary tale.

In 2006, Governor Arnold Schwarzenegger, global warming convert-turned-zealot, signed Assembly Bill 32 [AB 32] into law. Schwarzenegger—the same man who introduced Humvees to the commercial market—sought to bring the Golden State into compliance with the Kyoto Treaty. The draconian measure requires the state to reduce greenhouse gas emissions to their level in 1990, a nearly 25% reduction.

A mountain of red-tape restrictions and regulations are necessary to achieve the strict reduction goals in AB 32. The first victims of the regulations are the businesses that must lower their productivity in order to comply with the law. The second victims are the employees and consumers who rely upon those businesses. But in the global warming religion, these victims are really just sacrifices for the greater good of the planet—and they're not nearly as cute as polar bears.

Unable to remain solvent let alone profitable due to the excessive regulations and taxes, businesses are running for the state border. California faces over 12% unemployment and is projected to have a state deficit of $20 billion next year. For the first time since the Great Depression, the state issued IOU's to placate creditors until the previous budget crisis was resolved earlier this year.

Granted, not all of California's current problems can be attributed to AB 32 and other global warming hysteria-induced policies. But at a time when productivity is at an all-time low, real humans are being negatively impacted. As California teeters on the verge of disastrous bankruptcy, such feel-good environment laws are particularly damaging and illogical.

Forced to Make Unnecessary Sacrifices

The rest of America is not far behind California, as the federal government and states face similar financial ruin. But even in the shadow of impending doom, the climate change hysteria continues unabated. Global warming devotees continue to preach a gospel of sacrifice in order to "save" the planet.

In 2006 California governor Arnold Schwarzenegger signed Assembly Bill 32 into law. The measure requires the state to reduce greenhouse emissions by 25 percent, which the author argues hurts California economically.

Americans are no strangers to sacrifice. Americans have always sacrificed for something greater than themselves. In fact, like no other people in history, Americans have sacrificed their lives so that other nations could enjoy the very freedom the environmentalism tyranny seeks to steal.

Americans know when to sacrifice, but they also understand that certain kinds of sacrifice do not lead to productivity or freedom.

In order to combat climate change, we're told that we must cut back our energy usage. We're scolded out of our safe SUVs into fuel-efficient shoeboxes. We're admonished to take five minute showers or flush the toilet sparingly.

The practical effects of such rules? In California, certain kinds of televisions will be banned if they aren't energy efficient enough. The state legislature has considered allowing the government to directly control home thermostats. And the state legislature just approved an $11 billion water bond to address the state's water crisis.

FAST FACT

A 2007 Heartland Institute study claims that more than twenty-three years of temperature readings from satellites in the lower troposphere (an area scientists think would immediately reflect any global warming) have shown no warming. These readings, accurate to within 0.01°C, agree with data from weather balloons.

All of these restrictions and regulations are fundamentally un-American. Not because sacrifice or frugality are bad, but because this type of sacrifice is demanded in order to cover up government's mismanagement, or to achieve a purely political goal.

Choose Innovation over Environmentalism

Instead of mandating lower usage of resources, government should encourage private industry to find innovative ways to replace depleted resources. California's government has repeatedly defied attempts to produce clean nuclear energy or allow drilling off its coast. Finally taking on the state's critical need to build more dams and reservoirs, the legislature loaded the water bond with pork[1]; as much as half of the bond will go to non-water-related projects.

1. "Pork" is slang for unnecessary political initiatives that benefit political campaign contributors.

The only settled science (still denied by Democrats, liberals and progressives) is that government overregulation kills creativity, productivity and prosperity. Don't lower Americans' standard of living, unleash their creativity. Constantly demanding that man lower his expectations and quality of life reveals a belief that man cannot or should not achieve anything greater—that he must regress.

This type of thinking would never have allowed for President [John F.] Kennedy's ambitious space program—something that even then seemed an unachievable dream. But that "sky's the limit" vision enabled Americans to dream and aspire, and we achieved.

If the restrictive attitudes of global warming Chicken Littles had been shared by government leaders during our nation's times of great discovery, development and progress, we wouldn't have the incredible prosperity we now enjoy. A nation founded on liberty, limited government and boundless opportunity brought the greatest two centuries of modernization and progress in world history. Removing oppressive government environmental regulations—and stopping the cap-and-tax bill—will help turn around America's economy, and therefore the rest of the world.

World leaders should take to heart the old aphorism: A rising tide lifts all boats—and not just because the polar ice caps are melting.

EVALUATING THE AUTHOR'S ARGUMENTS:

In this viewpoint, Meredith Turney classifies attempts to get Americans to drive energy-efficient vehicles, buy energy-efficient products, and take shorter showers as "sacrifices." Do you agree? Are these sacrifices? Do they impinge on Americans' liberty? Why or why not, and do you think such measures are environmentally necessary?

Viewpoint 3

Threats to the Environment Are Real

Ruedigar Matthes

In the following viewpoint Ruedigar Matthes warns that environmental threats to the planet are real. He discusses a 2009 study that reviewed more than twenty-four thousand publications and concluded that habitat loss and species extinction are serious and growing threats. Worldwide, thousands of species have gone extinct or have been pushed to the brink of extinction, and thousands more are under threat from habitat loss, invasive species, or booming human populations. Matthes warns that the environment is being stressed to its limit by human-made factors such as overdevelopment and global warming. He concludes that humans are a part of nature, and if they do not take greater pains to protect the planet, they too shall suffer the consequences of environmental destruction.

Ruedigar Matthes writes about conservation and environmental issues for a variety of websites, including PlanetSave.com, which originally published this viewpoint.

"The threat to the environment is real. And for too long humankind has looked complacently on."

Ruedigar Matthes, "Invasive Species, Habitat Loss Threaten to Extinguish Life in Oceania," Planetsave.com, July 29, 2009. Reproduced by permission.

AS YOU READ, CONSIDER THE FOLLOWING QUESTIONS:

1. Who is Richard Kingsford and how does he factor into the author's argument?
2. By what percentage is Australia's population expected to increase by 2050?
3. How many of the world's forty-five thousand assessed species are threatened with extinction, according to Matthes?

It is estimated that man has been in Oceania for up to 125,000 years. The land was there before man. And for a long time a balance has been found between man and nature. Perhaps that balance was achieved because man and nature were not separate entities, but one and the same. However, in the recent past, that balance has been disturbed by population and consumption. Man became an invader rather than an aboriginal. And with that, habitat loss for other species has been a concern. And now life isn't what it used to be in Oceania.

It is such an invasion, not just by humans, but species of both flora and fauna that threatens aboriginal life in Oceania. A new study, which was published in the international journal *Conservation Biology* expresses the need for governments to act quickly in order to halt the loss of biodiversity and the extinction of species.

The study, which is the first comprehensive review of more than 24,000 scientific publications related to conservation in the Oceanic region, reveals the sad story of habitat destruction and species loss. It also offers a portrait of deficiencies and opportunities of regional and global governments as well as action that can be taken in order to front this mounting problem.

Mass Extinction Underway

"Earth is experiencing its sixth great extinction event and the new report reveals that this threat is advancing on six major fronts," says the report's lead author, Professor Richard Kingsford of the University of New South Wales.

Oceania is notorious for owning one of the world's worst extinction records. And the loss of species will continue unless there [are] "serious changes to the way we conserve our environments and dependent organisms," says Kingsford.

Humankind is a major contributing factor to such tragedy. The amazing natural environment in that region of the world is being destroyed by habitat loss and degradation, climate change, over-exploitation and pollution. Invasive species and wildlife disease also play a role in the extinguishment of life.

"Many people are just beginning to understand the full extent of these problems in terms of land-clearing, degradation of rivers, pest species and overfishing," says Professor Kingsford. "Climate change is a very important issue but by no means the only threat to biodiversity. The biggest problem seems to be that the policy challenges are just not

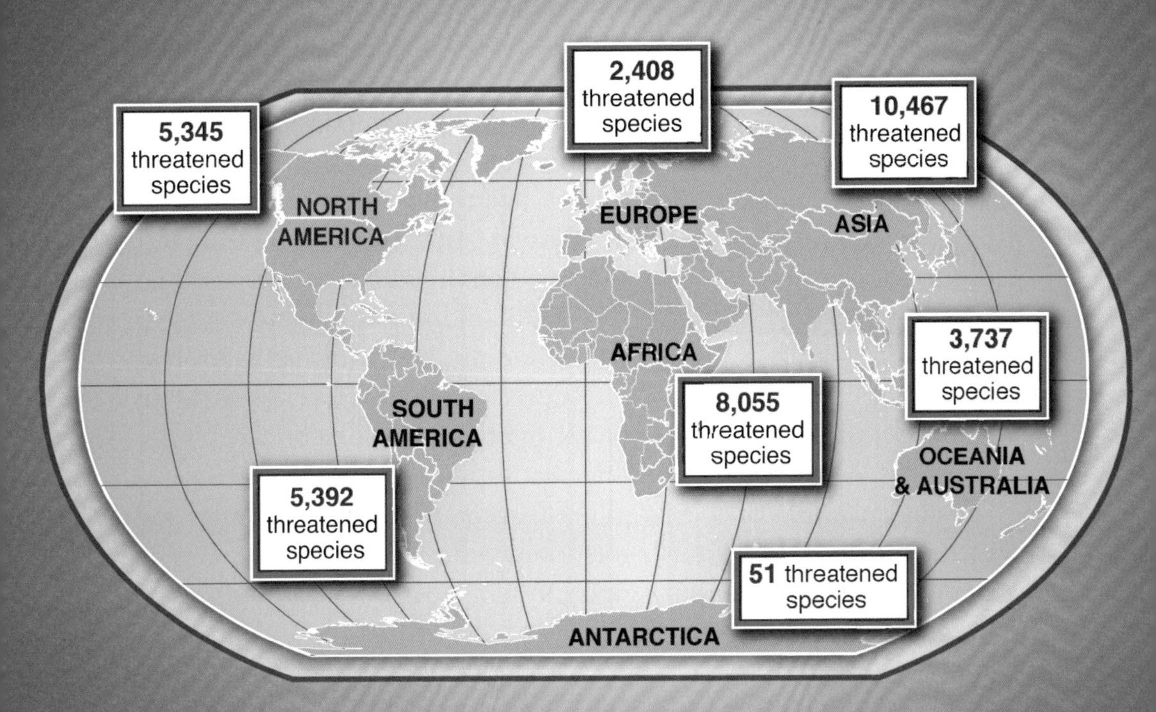

being taken up by governments. Conservation policies are just seen as a problem for the economy."

Conservation More Critical than Ever

Conservation has been pushed even farther under the bed of the global economic crisis. Despite the lack of attention given to conservation, Kinsford's team has not lost hope. For each of the major threats to biodiversity and conservation, the team has proposed between three and five specific policy recommendations that should be adopted by governments around the region.

Conservation is particularly important now because of the effects that human population has on the environment.

Populations in the region are predicted to increase significantly by 2050; for example Australia 35%; New Zealand 25%; Papua New Guinea 76%; New Caledonia 49%.

And with increased populations comes an increase in rubber-soled footprints. "The burden on the environment is going to get worse unless we are a lot smarter about reducing our footprint on the planet or the human population," says Professor Kingsford.

The threat to the environment is real. And for too long humankind has looked complacently on. Humankind has sat and watched while the earth around them has deteriorated. Why? Because it isn't happening to *them.* But what if the threat were to humankind's way of life? Would there be a different response?

The balance that once existed needs to be resurrected. "Unless we get this equation right, future generations will surely be paying more in terms of quality of life and the environment we live in," says Professor Kingsford.

Fast Fact

The Story of Stuff Project **states that 80 percent of the world's forests are gone, with the United States having less than 4 percent of its forests left. In the Amazon alone, two thousand trees—the equivalent of seven football fields—are cut down each minute. It is also estimated that 40 percent of the world's waterways are undrinkable.**

A tree kangaroo feeds in a forest in New Guinea. The loss and degradation of habitat is the largest single threat to land species.

To many ancient peoples, humankind was not *apart from* nature, but *a part of* nature. And while we have come to view ourselves otherwise, let us not forget that, in the end, extinction of fauna includes us.

Habitat Loss and Extinction Are Global Threats

Some findings in the report:

- Loss and degradation of habitat is the largest single threat to land species, including 80 percent of threatened species.
- More than 1,200 bird species have become extinct in the Pacific islands and archipelagos.

- In Australia agriculture has modified or destroyed about 50 percent of woodland and forest ecosystems, and about 70 percent of remaining forests are ecologically degraded from logging.
- Invasive species, particularly vertebrates and vascular plants, have devastated terrestrial species of the Pacific Islands and caused 75 percent of all terrestrial vertebrate extinctions on oceanic islands.
- More than 2,500 invasive plants have colonized New Zealand and Australia—representing about 11 percent of native plant species.
- Many invasive weeds, vertebrate pests, and fishes were introduced by government, agriculturalists, horticulturalists and hunters.
- Nearly 17,000 of the world's 45,000 assessed species are threatened with extinction (38 percent). Of these, 3,246 are in the highest category of threat, Critically Endangered, 4,770 are Endangered and 8,912 are Vulnerable to extinction.
- Nearly 5,500 animal species are known to be threatened with extinction and at least 1,141 of the 5,487 known mammal species are threatened worldwide.
- In 2008, nearly 450 mammals were listed as Endangered, including the Tasmanian Devil (*Sarcophilus harrisii*), after the global population declined by more than 60 percent in the last 10 years.
- Scientists have catalogued relatively little about the rest of the world's fauna: only 5 percent of fish, 6 percent of reptiles, and 7 percent of amphibians have been evaluated. Of those studied, at least 750 fish species, 290 reptiles, and 150 amphibians are at risk.
- The average extinction rate is now some 1,000 to 10,000 times faster than the rate that prevailed over the past 60 million years.

EVALUATING THE AUTHOR'S ARGUMENTS:

In this viewpoint Ruedigar Matthes claims that humans are integrally connected to nature and thus have a stake in its protection. He warns that extinction of species will eventually mean the extinction of humans, too. How do you think Bjørn Lomborg, author of the following viewpoint, might respond to this claim? Use examples from the texts you have read in your answer.

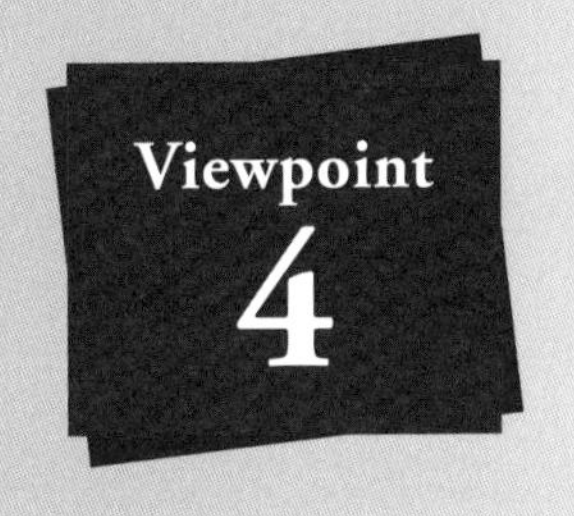

Environmentalists Exaggerate Threats to the Environment

Bjørn Lomborg

"More often than not, what sounds like horrific changes in climate and geography actually turns out to be quite manageable."

In the following viewpoint Bjørn Lomborg argues that threats to the environment are not as extreme as environmentalists claim. He says environmentalists greatly exaggerate the extent to which sea levels might rise as a result of global warming. They also overstate the effect such changes will have on human civilization. Lomborg says many cities have already responded to challenges posed by climate change, and have done so reasonably and with ease. In his opinion, there is no reason to think that future changes in the environment will be irreparable. Lomborg concludes that environmentalists trade in fear and hysteria, both of which impede innovative thinking and smart decision making regarding problems as complicated as climate change.

Bjørn Lomborg is a business professor, former director of the Environmental Assessment Institute in Copenhagen, Denmark, and the author of the book *The Skeptical Environmentalist.*

Bjørn Lomborg, "Sure, Worry About Climate Change—But Not Too Much," *Globe & Mail*, September 10, 2010.

AS YOU READ, CONSIDER THE FOLLOWING QUESTIONS:

1. By how many inches does Lomborg say global sea levels are likely to rise by 2100?
2. How does the author say the world might deal with a twenty-foot rise in sea levels?
3. What percentage of Britons does Lomborg say are "very concerned" about the environment?

For some years now, the debate over global warming has been dominated by fear. Understandably frustrated that their message might not be getting through, climate activists have been ratcheting up the rhetoric to the point where one could be excused for wondering whether they are quoting from scientific journals or the Book of Revelation. If nothing is done, we've been told, global warming would soon destroy "up to 40 per cent of the Amazonian forests," cut African crop yields in half by 2020, turn the American Southwest into a new dust bowl within a few decades and melt the Himalayan glaciers, causing them to disappear completely "by the year 2035 and perhaps sooner."

All very frightening, but none of it was based on solid science.

Dealing with Environmental Changes Reasonably

The chief Cassandra in this chorus of doom has been Al Gore, whose 2006 Oscar-winning documentary *An Inconvenient Truth* was unabashedly (and rather accurately) marketed as "the most terrifying film you will ever see." Mr. Gore rightly was awarded the 2007 Nobel Peace Prize for putting climate change on the global agenda, but his penchant for hyperbole—as in "we have just 10 years to avert a major catastrophe" or we must take "large-scale, preventative measures to protect human civilization as we know it"—isn't likely to win him any prizes for accuracy or good science.

Here's a case in point. Mr. Gore and his acolytes speak darkly of the likelihood that, because of global warming, sea levels may rise 15 or 20 feet over the next century. Let's put aside for the moment the fact that, according to the best research we have (from the UN's climate panel, which shared the Nobel Prize with Mr. Gore), global sea levels are not likely to rise more than about 20 inches by 2100—a level that history shows we can deal with quite easily. Rather, let's imagine that, over the next 80 or 90 years, a giant port city—say, Tokyo—found itself engulfed by a sea-level rise of the magnitude Mr. Gore suggests. It's a truly awful prospect, isn't it? Millions of inhabitants would be imperilled, along with trillions of dollars worth of infrastructure. Without a vast global effort, how could we possibly cope with such a terrifying catastrophe?

Well, we already have. In fact, we're doing it right now. Since 1930, excessive groundwater withdrawal has caused Tokyo to subside by as much as 15 feet. Similar subsidence has occurred over the past century in a vast range of cities, including Tianjin, Shanghai, Osaka, Bangkok and Jakarta. And in each case, the city has managed to protect itself from such large relative sea-level rises without much difficulty.

Environmentalists Greatly Exaggerate

The point isn't that we can or should ignore global warming. The point is that we should be wary of fear-mongering. More often than not, what sounds like horrific changes in climate and geography actually turns out to be quite manageable. In research funded by the

Opponents of climate change say Al Gore's documentary An Inconvenient Truth *was filled with exaggeration and scientific inaccuracy.*

European Union, climate scientists Robert J. Nicholls, Richard S.J. Tol and Athanasios T. Vafeidis recently studied what would happen in the unlikely event that the entire West Antarctic Ice Sheet collapsed. The result, they found, would be a sea-level rise of 20 feet over the next hundred years—exactly Mr. Gore's nightmare. But how calamitous would this really be?

Not very. According to these scientists, a 20-foot rise in sea levels would inundate about 16,000 square miles of coastline and affect more than 400 million people. That's a lot of people, to be sure, but it's hardly all of mankind. In fact, it amounts to less than 6 per cent of the world's population—which is to say that 94 per cent of the population would be unaffected. And most of those who do live in the flood areas wouldn't even get their feet wet. That's because the vast majority of those 400 million people reside within cities and other areas that could—and would—be protected relatively easily. (Remember Tokyo?) As a result, only about 15 million people would have to be relocated. And that's over the course of a century.

Fast Fact

Policy analysts James Plummer and Frances B. Smith claim that a modest amount of global warming would be beneficial to the natural world and to human civilization. Temperatures during the Medieval Warm Period (A.D. 800 to 1200), which led the Vikings to settle an inhospitable Greenland, were higher than today's worst-case scenario; 5000–3000 B.C., known as the "climatic optimum," was even warmer and allowed humans to focus on building civilizations.

The fact is, trying to scare the socks off people with end-of-the-world rhetoric doesn't make the world a better or safer place. Yes, a startling statistic combined with some hyperbolic prose will make us sit up and pay attention. But we quickly become desensitized, requiring ever more outrageous scenarios to move us. And as the scare stories grow more exaggerated, so, too, does the likelihood that they will be exposed for the exaggerations they are—and the public will end up tuning the whole thing out.

The Environment Is Not a Top Priority

A 2010 CNN poll asked Americans what they thought was the most important issue facing the country today. The environment was low on the list of national priorities.

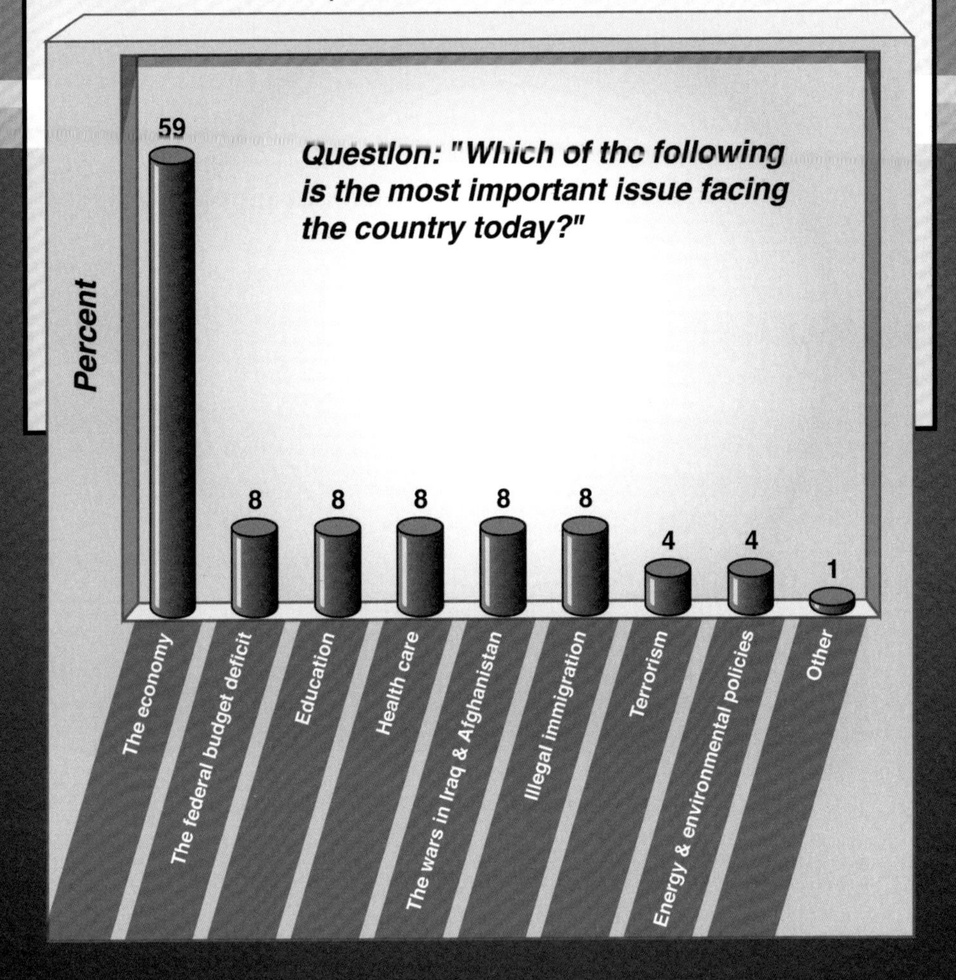

Taken from: CNN/Opinion Research Corporation Poll, October 27–30, 2010.

No Need for Fear

This may explain recent polling data showing that public concern about global warming has declined precipitously in recent years. For instance, a Gallup Poll found that the number of Americans who regard global warming as a serious problem has declined from 40 per cent in 2008 to just 32 per cent this year [2010]; the same poll also showed that the number of those who believe the seriousness of the problem has been greatly exaggerated has shot up from 30 per cent to 48 per cent over the past four years. Similarly, an Ipsos MORI poll published in the U.K. last June found that just 28 per cent of Britons are "very concerned" about climate change, down from 44 per cent five years ago. And in Germany, *Der Spiegel* magazine reported survey results showing that only 42 per cent feared global warming, compared with 62 per cent in 2006.

As these numbers imply, fear may be a great motivator, but it's a terrible basis for making smart decisions about a complicated problem that demands our full intelligence.

EVALUATING THE AUTHOR'S ARGUMENTS:

Bjørn Lomborg contends that most challenges posed by environmental change have a reasonable and relatively simple solution. How do you think the other authors in this chapter would respond to this claim? Write one to two sentences for each author, then state your position on the matter. Quote from the texts you have read in your answer.

All Americans Should Consider Themselves Environmentalists

Edward L. Glaeser

"We are all environmentalists now."

In the following viewpoint, Edward L. Glaeser argues that all Americans should consider themselves environmentalists because environmental problems threaten all Americans. He says environmentalism has shifted from being a liberal, flaky cause to a credible, all-encompassing movement that is best poised to tackle the number one problem humans face today: global warming. Glaeser says that innovators must think environmentally when they design new products; politicians must think environmentally when they legislate; and all citizens must think environmentally when they make choices that inform and affect everyday life. Glaeser concludes that climate change will impact all Americans, and thus all Americans have a stake in developing, innovating, and supporting environmental values.

Edward L. Glaeser is a professor of economics at Harvard University and the director of the Rappaport Institute for Greater Boston.

Edward L. Glaeser, "A Road Map for Environmentalism," *Boston Globe,* May 21, 2007. Reproduced by permission.

AS YOU READ, CONSIDER THE FOLLOWING QUESTIONS:

1. What does Glaeser say are three key elements of smart environmentalism?
2. In what way do patents hinder energy-efficient innovation, according to the author?
3. How does recycling paper hurt the environment, in Glaeser's opinion?

We are all environmentalists now. The growing threat posed by global warming makes it impossible to ignore the environmental impacts of our actions. No presidential candidate in 2008 will be able to act as if climate change is a loony leftist cause best fought with aggressive development of the Arctic.

But environmentalists should celebrate their much-deserved success with an increasing commitment to responsible policies that target climate change and weigh costs against benefits. In the early days of environmentalism, almost any action could be justified as a means of increasing environmental awareness. Now we are all aware and committed to the environment, and it is time to turn to policies that are both green and smart.

An Environmental Road Map

Smart environmentalism has three key elements. First, policies should be targeted toward the biggest environmental threat: global warming. Second, our resources and political capital are limited. This means we must weigh the benefits of each intervention against its costs. Third, we must anticipate unintended consequences, where being green in one place leads to decidedly non-green outcomes someplace else.

These simple rules provide a policy road map for environmentalism. The fight against climate change requires us to reduce greenhouse gas emissions. The most effective way to reduce emissions is to charge people for the social costs of their actions with a carbon tax. A significant carbon tax would be painful—gas will cost more at the pump—but it is never easy to change behavior, and change behavior we must.

The big challenge in reducing greenhouse gases is to reduce the growth of emissions in rapidly developing economies like China and India. I suspect this will require Europe and the United States to create incentives for these places to reduce emissions. One possible course of action is for American and European carbon taxes to provide funding that could be used to reward poorer countries for cutting emissions.

Smart Solutions

New technologies are likely to be our best weapons against climate change and we should try to encourage more energy-efficient innovation. Our patent system is poorly suited to encourage these innovations, since successful innovations will create environmental social benefits that far exceed the private revenues earned by the innovator. Patents also make it less likely that technology will be transferred to the developing world. A better system might be to offer large public prizes that reward innovations, which are then made freely available throughout the globe.

The author contends that Americans must think in terms of the environment when they make everyday choices.

But smart environmentalism doesn't just mean more government programs, it also means rethinking current policies. Our emissions policy, which requires regular emissions tests for newer vehicles, is expensive to operate and poorly designed to fight climate change. After all, it does nothing to induce less driving. Even more problematically, by letting owners of older cars off the hook, the current system imposes costs on the Prius driver but exempts the drivers of the vintage gas guzzlers that create the most emissions. We should require different emissions tests and even higher emission taxes for older cars that generate higher environmental costs.

Fast Fact

According to a 2009 National Wildlife Federation poll, 84 percent of American voters consider environmental issues to be a "high" priority in presidential elections. Further, four out of five Americans consider themselves to be environmentalists or sympathetic to environmentalists.

Our paper recycling programs cost time and money and do little to protect first-growth woodlands and rain forests. The trees used by paper mills are a renewable resource. When people use more paper, suppliers plant more trees. If we want bigger commercial forests, then we should use more paper, not less. Our policies should directly protect important wildlife habitats, not try to reduce our demand for paper.

Climate Change Affects Us All

Perhaps the most environmentally problematic local policies are land-use controls. The foes of development correctly point out that new development will use energy and land, but the right calculation also considers the costs created by stopping development and pushing it elsewhere. When we stop development in Boston's inner-ring suburbs, we shift development to areas with fewer people that might oppose new development. The move from higher- to lower-density development ensures more driving and energy use. Protecting green space in the inner suburbs is a form of environmentalism, but it is an environmentalism that creates local benefits by imposing costs on the rest of the world, since it pushes development into the highway-crazy exurbs.

The state should take the lead by requiring environmental impact reviews to compare the environmental costs of allowing a project with the expected environmental consequences if a rejected project is built elsewhere.

Climate change is too important for us not to consider all of the consequences of our policies. We should rethink policies that appear environmental but that actually ensure more driving and greenhouse gases.

EVALUATING THE AUTHOR'S ARGUMENTS:

In this viewpoint Edward L. Glaeser uses facts, examples, and reasoning to argue that all Americans have a stake in protecting the environment. He does not, however, use any quotations to support his points. If you were to rewrite this article and insert quotations, what authorities might you quote from? Where would you place them, and why?

Environmentalism Is for Privileged, White Americans

"These controversies . . . are uncomfortably whitewashed, and the only people we hear from are middle-class individuals with the privilege to choose environmentally friendly lifestyles."

Jeremy R. Levine

In the following viewpoint Jeremy R. Levine argues that environmentalism is a boutique cause most easily embraced by privileged, white, middle-class Americans. He discusses how public transportation debates in certain American cities have come to focus less on who needs to use mass transit to get where, and why, and instead on how such transit can transform America into a green, eco-friendly nation. He says it is easy for white middle-class Americans to trade their cars for bikes or walking, because most of these people live in safe suburban neighborhoods where they both live and work. But Levine points out that poor, urban people of color are less likely to live in such places. They rely on public transportation not to live a feel-good, emission-free lifestyle but rather to help them bridge the great distance between their urban home and suburban job. Levine concludes that environmental policies tend to best suit white, middle-class, privileged Americans, which in his opinion is unfair and even racist.

Jeremy R. Levine, "Environmentalism is Political White Privilege," socialsciencelite.blogspot.com, June 5, 2009. Reproduced by permission.

Jeremy R. Levine is a graduate student in the Department of Sociology at Harvard University and a doctoral fellow in the Multidisciplinary Program in Inequality and Social Policy at Harvard's John F. Kennedy School of Government.

AS YOU READ, CONSIDER THE FOLLOWING QUESTIONS:

1. What is the black male unemployment rate, according to Levine?
2. What does "spatial mismatch" mean as used by the author?
3. What does the term "whitewashed" mean as Levine uses it?

PBS [the Public Broadcasting Service] ran a special on suburban sprawl last week [in May 2009] entitled "Blueprint America: Road to the Future." The special profiled three U.S. cities—Denver, Portland and New York City—taking three very different approaches to metropolitan transit.

Environmentalism Laden with White Privilege

The special began with Denver and local political battles over a nearly complete highway enclosing the region. Opponents of the highway suggested that it contributes to sprawl and is decimating the environment, while proponents made the groundbreaking observation "Our population is increasing, and they have to live somewhere!" Basically, metro-Denver residents are dependent on their cars due to greedy real estate developers, federal subsidies for suburban development, and a general American "car culture." And this dependency has had dramatic effects on the area's quality of life and air quality. Thirty-minute rush hour commutes now take upwards of two hours, meaning more carbon emissions and more pollution.

Portland was profiled next as a region bucking the trend of suburban sprawl. When the city was offered federal dollars for highway construction in the 1970s, city officials instead invested in light rails and other public transit systems. White, middle-class families were followed with cameras as they rode their bikes to the local grocery store and then to a neighborhood playground. Under Mayor

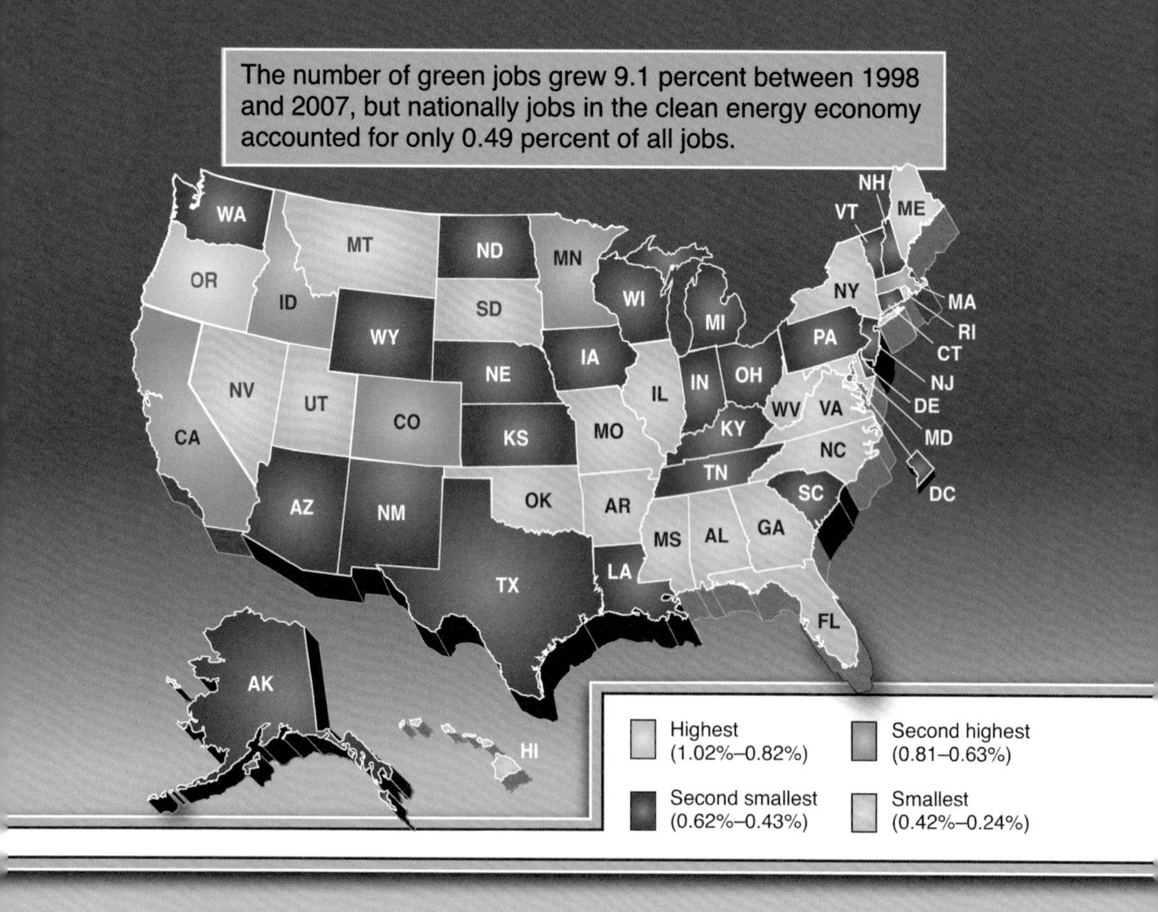

Taken from: Pew Charitable Trusts, 2009, based on the National Establishment Time Scenes Database; analysis by Pew Center on the States and Collaborative Economics.

[Michael] Bloomberg, New York City—already very "green" by emissions standards—is following Portland and also making environmental sustainability a civic priority.

The common thread throughout the entire special was twofold: Sprawl has dramatically negative effects on the environment, and better transit is necessary if we want to be a "green," eco-friendly nation. White, middle-class families in Portland were quoted in the special gleefully recounting how they can ride their bikes to work, instead of driving. But what about folks that don't even have cars? What about folks who live in neighborhoods spatially disconnected from job opportunities? These controversies over public transportation are uncomfortably whitewashed, and the only people we hear from are middle-class individuals with *the privilege to choose environmentally friendly lifestyles.* Here we are, debating the best way to commute to work, when black male unemployment is 17.2%.

All Jobs Are Needed, Not Just "Green Jobs"

This discussion brings up the idea of framing—how we talk about social issues. The [Barack] Obama Administration's head of The Department of Transportation was quoted in the PBS special [as] saying, "We're thinking about transit more than ever before." But *how* are they thinking about it? Are they thinking about it as a political move, a way to garner support from "green loving" liberals? Or is the conversation more altruistic—a way to help the country recover from the economic crisis? Or—and here's where things get interesting—can it be positioned as a social justice, a social need for already marginalized urban communities?

In *Lone Pursuit,* Sandra Susan Smith—a brilliant sociologist at UC–Berkeley—discusses black joblessness in southeast Michigan, carefully analyzing job referral reluctance among poor African Americans. A cycle of distrust proliferates among the black poor in "Southeast County," Michigan, thwarting the dissemination of job information through informal networks. She posits that a weak job referral structure at the *individual* level in Southeast County helps explain low employment levels for blacks at the *group* level.

Fast Fact

According to environmental attorney Richard Ayres, the Conservation Movement in the late nineteenth and early twentieth centuries was considered an elitist movement. It consisted of a few wealthy gentlemen who had visited lush nature sites and wanted to protect them.

Throughout the book, however, her respondents also noted the trials and tribulations associated with mass transit. Indeed, this is a hot topic in Southeast Michigan. Currently, state officials are split on plans to build a commuter rail from "Southeast County" (Ann Arbor/

The author argues that lower-income Americans who live far from job centers do not have the luxury of biking to work or buying fuel-efficient vehicles.

Ypsilanti) to either Detroit or Grand Rapids. Representatives from Grand Rapids are seeking to make their city the "center" of the state, whereas Detroit representatives are simply trying to keep their city alive. And, of course, poor folks just want a job, and a way to get there.

This is also a nationwide problem; social scientists term it "spatial mismatch." The idea is that the place of employment is divorced from a group or individual's place of residence. In metropolitan America, work has "disappeared" to the suburbs via decentralization, while poor, predominantly black city residents remain constrained to residence within city limits. See, this is what's missing from conversations about transportation policy, environmental sustainability and suburban sprawl. Poor people, particularly in marginalized communities of color, need jobs and a reliable way to get to them. Lofty goals of "going green" are well and good, but we also need better public transit for *the employment opportunities of the public.*

A Whitewashed Worldview Solves Nothing

In the aftermath of the financial crisis, a plethora of media outlets have profiled newly unemployed whites from corporate America.

Coupled with the conversations of environmentalism and mass transit, it appears that the public conception of the economy has been effectively whitewashed. The effects of sprawl are more than simply environmental, and the need for mass transit is bigger than the quality of life for middle-class whites in Portland. We can't allow our privilege to get in the way of seeing who really needs public transit, and why they need it.

EVALUATING THE AUTHOR'S ARGUMENTS:

Jeremy R. Levine argues that environmentally friendly mass transit is being designed to favor privileged, middle-class Americans rather than the poorer, working-class individuals who need it most. Do you agree with him that transportation and other environmental initiatives, such as recycling or using solar power, are most easily embraced by individuals who have the luxury of choosing environmentally friendly lifestyles? Or, do you think the whole of society stands to gain from environmentally friendly policies and initiatives? Explain your reasoning.

Chapter 2

Is Environmentalism Good for Society?

Proponents of environmental legislation say that such laws will help create environmentally friendly jobs, while opponents argue that such laws will cause jobs to be cut.

Environmentalism Is Good for the Economy

"National renewable energy and energy efficiency standards will drive demand for new products and services, which will then stand up the industries needed to create jobs."

Van Jones

In the following viewpoint Van Jones argues that transitioning to alternative sources of energy will save money, create jobs, and boost the economy. Jones argues that investing in environmentally friendly technologies will create a "green economy," one that is based on cutting-edge skills and technologies that will put millions of unemployed Americans back to work. These workers will receive valuable training that will provide them with modern skills; at the same time, contends Jones, the greening of America will save money in a variety of sectors. Jones imagines an America in which solar and wind power, green building construction, homegrown biofuel production, and environmental initiatives like planting trees and recycling waste will give millions of American workers high-paying domestic jobs that cannot be outsourced overseas. For all these reasons he concludes that environmental initiatives can be good for the American economy.

An environmental advocate and attorney, Van Jones was appointed by President

Van Jones, "Speaking of 'Small People': Will the Energy Bill Hurt or Help Them?," *Center for American Progress,* June 18, 2010. This material was created by the Center for American Progress. www.americanprogress.org.

Barack Obama as the first special adviser for green jobs, enterprise, and innovation. He served in this position from March to September 2009. He is also the author of *The Green Collar Economy.*

AS YOU READ, CONSIDER THE FOLLOWING QUESTIONS:

1. The United States is home to how many unemployed construction workers, according to Jones?
2. In what way does the author think green energy policies could help poor and rural American farmers and landowners?
3. How will national renewable energy and energy efficiency standards drive demand for new products and services, according to Jones?

A BP executive got himself in hot water this week for suggesting that his company is not "greedy" and cares about the "small people." Pundits were outraged less by his lies than by his condescension.

Admittedly, he should have chosen a different phrase to describe the low-income and vulnerable Americans who are suffering in the gulf region. But he was right to put concern for their plight at the center of the debate.

The question is: Will clean energy champions do the same thing? After all, we know that the dirty energy spill hurt vulnerable Americans. But will the clean energy bill help them?

The time has come to call the question. Momentum is again gathering for comprehensive clean energy and climate legislation. The EPA analysis of the Kerry-Lieberman American Power Act looks promising, lowering consumer costs and creating badly needed jobs. President Barack Obama's Oval Office speech made the case. July looks to be the month for historic action.

As we move forward, how can we ensure that legislation will bring real and tangible benefits to low-income communities? Any piece of energy legislation should protect the lowest-income consumers from higher energy bills while also creating real jobs and economic opportunities in vulnerable communities. Put another way, such proposals should minimize the pain and maximize the gain.

Our nation deserves an American Power Act that empowers all Americans. And those communities that were left behind and hurt in the old, pollution-based economy should be lifted up and helped in the new, clean, and green economy.

Overall, the present version of the American Power Act is quite promising. It does include some strong provisions to lower consumer costs and provide access to new clean energy jobs. But it lacks some fundamental provisions to truly scale up the clean energy economy, ensure that green jobs are good jobs, and put some green rungs on the ladder out of poverty.

The Good Stuff

Positive: Jobs, Workforce Development, and Access

Much of what is strong in the bill reflects the dedication of the bill's sponsors—and the good, hard work of Green For All, the Climate Equity Alliance, the Apollo Alliance, and other dedicated advocates.

The clean energy economy has the potential to unlock numerous employment opportunities for disadvantaged and underrepresented communities. These jobs respect the environment and also offer opportunities for dignified work that lifts people out of poverty and provides access to the middle class.

This opportunity is particularly important to the nation's 2.1 million unemployed construction workers—where sectors such as residential construction have unemployment rates as high as 38 percent.

One major provision in the bill, the Green Construction Careers Demonstration Project, will bring some relief to unemployed construction workers and provide access to some job seekers who otherwise might be left out of these jobs—including women and people of color. The construction sector and other related industries—such as manufacturers of construction equipment and materials—will experience significant growth as a result of this increased investment by the federal government.

The purpose of the Demonstration Project is "to promote middle class careers and quality employment practices in the green construction sector among targeted workers and to advance efficiency and performance on construction projects." Projects in the demonstration area are required to have a minimum portion of hours worked by

The Green Economy

The growth of renewable energy industries is expected to create new jobs that will pay well and be available for outsourcing.

Industry	Job Opportunities
Building Retrofitting	Electricians, Heating/Air Conditioning Installers, Carpenters, Construction Equipment Operators, Roofers, Insulation Workers, Carpenter Helpers, Industrial Truck Drivers, Construction Managers, Building Inspectors
Mass Transit/ Freight Rail	Civil Engineers, Rail Track Layers, Electricians, Welders, Metal Fabricators, Engine Assemblers, Bus Drivers, Dispatchers, Locomotive Engineers, Railroad Conductors
Smart Grid	Computer Software Engineers, Electrical Engineers, Electrical Equipment Assemblers, Electrical Equipment Technicians, Machinists, Team Assemblers, Construction Laborers, Operating Engineers, Electrical Power Line Installers and Repairers
Wind Power	Environmental Engineers, Iron and Steel Workers, Millwrights, Sheet Metal Workers, Machinists, Electrical Equipment Assemblers, Construction Equipment Operators, Industrial Truck Drivers, Industrial Production Managers, First-Line Production Supervisors
Solar Power	Electrical Engineers, Electricians, Industrial Machinery Mechanics, Welders, Metal Fabricators, Electrical Equipment Assemblers, Construction Equipment Operators, Installation Helpers, Laborers, Construction Managers
Advanced Biofuels	Chemical Engineers, Chemists, Chemical Equipment Operators, Chemical Technicians, Mixing and Blending Machine Operators, Agriculture Workers, Industrial Truck Drivers, Farm Product Purchasers, Agricultural and Forestry Supervisor, Agricultural Inspectors

Taken from: University of Massachusetts Amherst Political Economy Research Institute & the Center for American Progress September 2008 Green Recovery report.

members of targeted groups. This means that low-income workers, women, and people of color will have a fair chance at accessing decent construction jobs that pay well, can support a family, and have helped many Americans gain access to the middle class.

The Green Construction Demonstration Project also establishes that each contractor and subcontractor on construction projects in the program must participate in a qualified labor-management apprenticeship program, with a qualified pre-apprenticeship program, for each craft and trade. Apprentice and pre-apprentice programs are a big deal for workers because they receive on-the-job training while still getting paid.

The program also allows the secretary of labor to create community workforce agreements that establish uniform labor and workplace safety standards, as well as coordinate and reinforce the targeted hiring goals and training programs. These are important because they provide worker protection agreements that ensure that workplaces are safe and workers are treated fairly.

Finally, the bill authorizes Clean Energy Curriculum Development Grants for eligible community partners—such as community colleges—to develop education programs for emerging careers in the clean energy economy. These are the kinds of training programs that all people, including disadvantaged groups, can access in their own communities. It would allow them to receive training in lots of different sectors of the clean energy economy—including green-construction, clean manufacturing, renewable energy, forestry, sustainable agriculture, and climate change mitigation. It also requires the secretaries of labor, energy, and education to develop web-based information and resources for career and technical education and job training in the renewable energy sector.

All these provisions are important because they create pathways to middle-class jobs for all communities, including low-income Americans, women, and communities of color.

Positive: Consumer Protection Against Rising Energy Costs

The proposed American Power Act includes important measures to minimize the pain and assist low- and moderate-income families in meeting their basic energy needs—including both electricity and home heating oil. These households will receive direct payments in the form of refunds and direct rebates. The refunds are large enough to protect households in the poorest 20 percent of the population from feeling financial hardship as a result of rising energy prices.

It is important to note that energy prices are not expected to rise significantly as a result of climate legislation. In fact, analysis shows that it will actually save families $35 per year through 2020, and more than $71 per year by 2025. In the short run, however, even a small rise in the cost of energy can have significant impact for those in the lowest income households—which is why these measures are important.

Here are some additional details about the refund program that the Center on Budget and Policy Priorities has outlined:

- Households with incomes at or below 150 percent of the poverty line will be eligible to receive monthly energy refunds by direct deposit or through states' electronic benefit transfer systems—the debit card systems states use to deliver food stamps and other federal benefits.
- Households that receive food stamps, as well as low-income seniors and people with disabilities who participate in the Supplemental Security Income program, will be automatically enrolled for energy refunds. Other households will have to apply for refunds.
- Households with slightly higher incomes—between 150 and 250 percent of the poverty line, or about $33,000 to $55,000 for a family of four—will be eligible for a smaller tax credit.

It is important that our commitment to fight climate change and realize a new clean energy economy does not disproportionately affect poor and vulnerable communities, who pay the highest portion of their income toward energy bills.

Positive: Opportunity for Rural America

The American Power Act includes opportunities for poor farmers and other rural Americans to access new sources of revenue and jobs, and implement clean energy and energy efficiency on their lands.

The bill will support the Rural Energy for America Program, which helps farmers, ranchers, and rural small businesses with grants that will allow them to install clean energy resources on their lands and cut energy waste by implementing energy efficiency upgrades.

The bill also will establish a multibillion dollar domestic offset program, which will pay farmers and other landowners to plant extra trees to absorb carbon dioxide, install methane capture systems for animal waste, or store carbon in the soil.

Shifting to a clean energy economy on rural lands makes sense for rural America, where large portions of the population live in poverty and unemployment. And the measures outlined above will triple potential revenue streams for farmers and rural communities.

What Needs Improvement in the American Power Act

It perhaps goes without saying that the Senate proposal could be much stronger or more aggressive in cutting carbon. I will focus my comments on the economic impacts and areas of need.

Needed: "Green Jobs Act" Funding for Job Training

Funding for the Green Jobs Act is one of the bigger provisions left out of the current Senate bill, although it is included in the House version. This is a disappointing miss and a big loss for millions of the nation's job seekers.

The Green Jobs Act, which President George W. Bush signed into law in 2007, authorized $125 million in green-collar job training opportunities. That's enough money to train about 30,000 workers a year for jobs in emerging "green" sectors such as the solar and wind industries, green building construction, biofuel production, and more. The American Recovery and Reinvestment Act (ARRA, the so-called "stimulus bill") allocated $500 million in one-time funding to the Green Jobs Act. Happily, the version of the climate bill that passed the House last summer did incorporate support for the Green Jobs Act. But this important program is not included in the present version of the American Power Act.

> **FAST FACT**
>
> **A 2007 poll by the Center for American Progress found that 79 percent of Americans said they believe shifting to alternative forms of energy can help America's economy and create jobs.**

Many low-income workers will not be able to fully participate in the job creation spurred by this bill without equitable access to training opportunities.

Needed: Stronger Labor Standards

Another disappointing provision left out of the Senate bill, also included in the House version, is compliance with Davis-Bacon wage requirements. Davis-Bacon provides assurances that prevailing wages will be paid at minimum to all laborers and mechanics employed by contractors or subcontractors on construction projects funded by the federal government. It is a clear legislative way to ensure that new green jobs are also new good jobs.

Needed: Incentives for "Made in America" Clean Energy

Without real incentives for "made in America" clean energy, there may not be enough green manufacturing jobs to make a dent in our unemployment rate—let alone to create opportunity on a broad scale.

One of the major questions that still remain about America's clean energy policy is whether it will include a strong national renewable energy and energy efficiency standard. These are national goals to achieve a set amount of our nation's energy from renewable sources such as the wind and the sun. There can also be goals for the amount of energy we save—for instance, by taking measures like switching out energy-wasting light bulbs, replacing leaky windows and doors, and new insulation. At this point, these national goals are not spelled out clearly—but they should be. We should strive for a national renewable energy standard that requires 25 percent of electricity to be produced from clean energy by 2025 and an energy efficiency standard of 10 percent energy savings through efficiency upgrades by 2020.

National renewable energy and energy efficiency standards will drive demand for new products and services, which will then stand up the industries needed to create jobs. They will create the family-supporting, well-paying jobs that have helped many Americans gain access to the middle class.

Such standards would help spur manufacturing of clean energy technology—and create green-collar jobs—in the United States. Investors and companies would be able to see clear and concrete goals for deploying new technologies in our country—and pour private capital into these new industries. That would create jobs. Without a strong, national renewable energy goal, most green manufacturing will take place in other countries, which will get the bulk of the world's green jobs as a result.

Van Jones speaks in Cleveland, Ohio, at a conference on environmental issues. Jones was appointed by President Barack Obama to serve as special adviser for green jobs, enterprise, and innovation.

In addition to a national renewable energy and efficiency standards, a clean energy and climate bill must provide additional incentives for companies to invest in clean energy technologies. Extending manufacturing tax credits and grants for clean energy development will spur the necessary investment in clean energy technologies required to bring them to a large and meaningful scale.

The present version of the bill does not provide enough incentives to spur sufficient investment in the development and deployment of energy efficiency and clean energy on a large enough scale that could meet America's power needs.

Conclusion

BP's "small people" comment caused Americans to roll their eyes, in part because we know better than to expect a big oil company to care about vulnerable people. But we do expect Congress to care. And we expect our leaders to translate that concern into strong legislation that actively protects and promotes the interests of the most vulnerable Americans.

Clean energy and climate legislation should blunt the drain on consumers' wallets and accelerate the gain in creating jobs and building up industries to create a pathway to prosperity. The proposed American Power Act represents a good start, with important programs for the nation's low-income and undeserved communities. Yet the proposed legislation is far from complete. Fortunately, the U.S. Senate has a great opportunity to strengthen the bill by adding these important missing elements.

EVALUATING THE AUTHOR'S ARGUMENTS:

Van Jones argues that imposing energy standards on the nation's industries will put people back to work, spur investment, and help new industries thrive. Loren B. Thompson, author of the following viewpoint, disagrees, arguing that government-imposed standards hinder industry and kill jobs. After reading both viewpoints, with which author do you agree, and why? List at least two pieces of evidence that swayed you.

Environmentalism Is Bad for the Economy

Loren B. Thompson

"Environmentalists are . . . strangling the ability of local economies to prosper."

Environmentalism hampers economic growth and limits job creation, argues Loren B. Thompson in the following viewpoint. He discusses how environmental regulations have cut people off from their land and forced companies to operate with one hand tied behind their back. The activism of environmentalists, he claims, has resulted in fines, obstructions, or other impositions that have made companies unable to hire new workers or have even forced them to leave the United States. For these reasons he concludes that environmentalism is bad for the economy and urges Americans to reject environmental regulations.

Loren B. Thompson is chief operating officer of the Lexington Institute, a public policy organization that opposes federal intervention in commerce and culture.

AS YOU READ, CONSIDER THE FOLLOWING QUESTIONS:

1. Why was a large swath of Plymouth Beach, Massachusetts, rendered inaccessible to residents, according to Thompson?
2. How have environmentalists been active in North Carolina, according to the author?
3. What country does Thompson say has benefited from America's strict environmental regulations?

Loren B. Thompson, "Environmental Extremism Threatens Economy, Security—and Environmentalism," *Lexington Institute,* October 25, 2010.

Every few months I visit the Massachusetts town my mother's immigrant family came to a hundred years ago in search of work at the textile mills which dotted the New England coast. Like many municipalities near Boston, Plymouth is a fairly cosmopolitan place where people listen to National Public Radio and usually vote for Democrats. But recently I've begun to notice one issue typically associated with progressive voters falling out of favor—environmentalism. That's surprising, because Plymouth residents used to be so environmentally conscious that they drove [cranberry conglomerate] Ocean Spray's headquarters out of town rather than let the company fill in a small portion of the bay.

Environmental Regulations Hurt Local Industry

But something has changed in their opinions about the environment, or at least about environmentalists, and I know what it is. Several years ago, a wealthy woman from California bought a house on the beach and tried to limit vehicles going by her land. Plymouth Beach is a peninsula, so if you can't get by her house, half of the beach is beyond reach. The dispute has grown quite arcane, but part of her reasoning is that nesting migratory birds in the area might be adversely affected by vehicles, even if the vehicles stay in carefully demarcated routes. The case is still in litigation, but Plymouth Beach now has multiple checkpoints manned by the local equivalent of park rangers, and vehicle access to the upper beach is carefully controlled. This angers residents who have been driving up the beach their whole lives, but who now face the prospect of having their vehicles permanently banned.

Fast Fact

The American Policy Roundtable claims that reducing US carbon dioxide emissions to 7 percent below 1990 levels by the year 2012—the target set by the Kyoto Protocol—would require higher energy taxes, with regulations that would cause the nation to lose 2.4 million jobs and $300 billion in annual economic output.

The reason you should care about this little vignette from a place that likes to call itself "America's hometown" is that similar stories are

This photo shows lean soil studded with holes caused by the mining of rare-earth metals in Jiangxi Province, China. California formerly produced rare earths, but antienvironmentalists contend that state regulations killed the industry, giving China a monopoly on rare-earth mining.

playing out all over America. In North Carolina, environmentalists want to block a foreign company's effort to build one of the biggest cement plants in the U.S., because they say it has not conducted sufficient studies of the plant's environmental impact. The company says the requested studies are redundant and unnecessary. In Idaho, environmentalists are challenging a Canadian oil company's plan to move giant Korean mining rigs from the coast inland over the one local road that doesn't have tunnels or overpasses. They say the company isn't prepared to deal with accidents on the remote road. In California, environmentalists want even tighter controls on the presence of a rocket-fuel ingredient called perchlorate in ground water. The company responsible for the cleanup says it has already reduced levels of the chemical to a few parts per billion—far below the level at which the Environmental Protection Agency's inspector general says human effects disappear.

The Economy Is More Important than the Environment

A 2010 poll found that more Americans think economic growth should be the country's priority, even if the environment suffers. Older Americans, Republicans, and independents were more likely to think this than Democrats and younger Americans, however.

Question: "With which one of these statements about the environment and the economy do you most agree? Protection of the environment should be given priority, even at the risk of curbing economic growth. Or, economic growth should be given priority, even if the environment suffers to some extent."

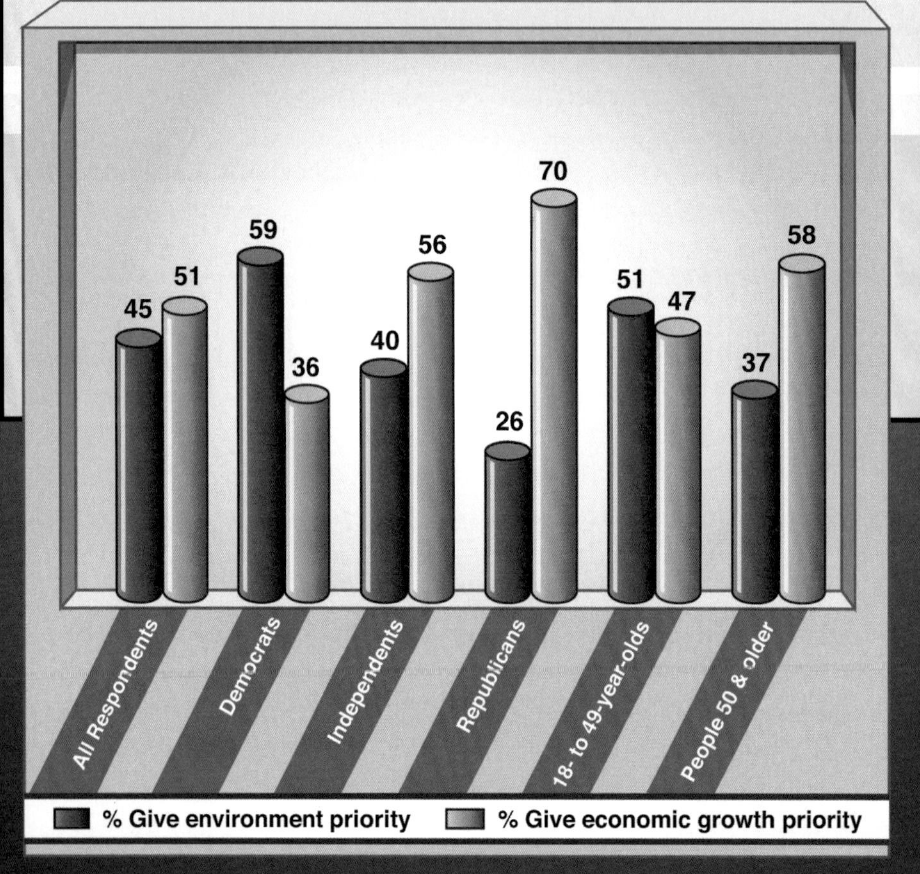

* numbers do not add up to 100% because small percentages of respondents said both should get equal priority, or that they were unsure.

Taken from: Opinion Research Corporation Poll, March 19–21, 2010.

Environmentalism Strangles the Economy

All over America, people who once enthusiastically supported the environmental movement are beginning to have doubts. They see that in many cases, there is no limit to the demands environmentalists are willing to make on industry, and that as a result they are strangling the ability of local economies to prosper. They also notice that the people backing heavy environmental regulation often are college-educated, affluent folks who won't really be affected by the rules, whereas the people whose livelihoods are on the line are less educated and less affluent. Consequently, environmentalism is gradually losing the hold it once had on many voters.

It's no secret that whole industries have been driven out of America by tougher environmental rules. China and other countries with less onerous regulations have benefited handsomely from this migration. For instance, a single mine in California once met most of the world's needs for vital rare earths used in everything from radars to mobile phones, but just about the time it started to encounter low-cost Chinese competition, it also ran afoul of environmental agencies. End result: the mine closed in 2002, and China now has a global monopoly in the production of rare earths. Such stories suggest that like many other revolutions in history, environmentalism has entered the stage of excess and extremism where it destroys its own success. If environmentalists can't find some way of curbing their propensity for endless litigation and rule-making, they eventually will be overwhelmed by popular revolt against their self-righteous obstructionism.

EVALUATING THE AUTHOR'S ARGUMENTS:

Loren B. Thompson argues that environmental regulations particularly threaten poor, less-educated people. Van Jones, author of the previous viewpoint, argues that poor, uneducated people have the most to gain from environmental innovations. After reading both viewpoints, what do you think about whether environmentalism helps or hurts poor people? Quote from the texts you have read in your answer.

Environmentalism Is a Threat to Society

Keith Lockitch

"It is hard for us to project the degree of sacrifice and harm that proposed climate policies would force upon us."

In the following viewpoint Keith Lockitch explains why he thinks environmentalism is a threat to society. He views environmentalists as anti-progress, anti-technology, and thus anti-civilization. Lockitch explains that environmentalists think humans should relinquish energy sources that negatively impact the earth, such as fossil fuels like gas, oil, and coal. But, according to Lockitch, these energy sources serve a variety of critical functions, including keeping hospitals running, facilitating global travel, and keeping people warm, fed, and safe. Lockitch believes that by demanding that people drastically cut their fossil fuel use, environmentalists seek to undermine human achievement and progress. He suggests that environmentalists do not fully comprehend that if society actually adopted their policies, human civilization would slip catastrophically backwards. He thus concludes environmentalism represents a threat to society.

Keith Lockitch holds a doctorate degree in physics and is a resident fellow at the Ayn Rand Institute, where he focuses on science and environmentalism.

Keith Lockitch, "The Real Meaning of Earth Hour," Ayn Rand Institute, March 23, 2009. Reproduced by permission.

AS YOU READ, CONSIDER THE FOLLOWING QUESTIONS:

1. What is "Earth Hour," as described by Lockitch?
2. What "comforting-but-false" message does the author say is sent by Earth Hour?
3. What do city lights symbolize to Lockitch?

On Saturday, March 28, [2009] cities around the world will turn off their lights to observe "Earth Hour." Iconic landmarks from the Sydney Opera House to Manhattan's skyscrapers will be darkened to encourage reduced energy use and signal a commitment to fighting climate change.

Las Vegas, Nevada, was one of the world's cities that celebrated Earth Hour by turning off lights for an hour (top photo) as a call to action on climate change.

While a one-hour blackout will admittedly have little effect on carbon emissions, what matters, organizers say, is the event's symbolic meaning. That's true, but not in the way organizers intend.

Environmentalists Want People to Renounce Society

We hear constantly that the debate is over on climate change—that man-made greenhouse gases are indisputably causing a planetary emergency. But there is ample scientific evidence to reject the claims of climate catastrophe. And what's never mentioned? The fact that reducing greenhouse gases to the degree sought by climate activists would, itself, cause significant harm.

Politicians and environmentalists, including those behind Earth Hour, are not calling on people just to change a few light bulbs, they are calling for a truly massive reduction in carbon emissions—as much as 80 percent *below* 1990 levels. Because our energy is overwhelmingly carbon-based (fossil fuels provide more than 80 percent of world energy), and because the claims of abundant "green energy" from breezes and sunbeams are a myth—this necessarily means a massive reduction in our energy use.

Fast Fact

According to the Heritage Foundation, fuel economy and emissions standards for passenger cars, light-duty trucks, and medium-duty passenger vehicles will cost the auto industry $10.8 billion per year for model years 2012 to 2016.

People don't have a clear view of what this would mean in practice. We, in the industrialized world, take our abundant energy for granted and don't consider just how much we benefit from its use in every minute of every day. Driving our cars to work and school, sitting in our lighted, heated homes and offices, powering our computers and countless other labor-saving appliances, we count on the indispensable values that industrial energy makes possible: hospitals and grocery stores, factories and farms, international travel and global telecommunications. It is hard for us to project the degree of sacrifice and harm that proposed climate policies would force upon us.

Americans Think Jobs, the Budget, Health Care, and Taxes Are More Crucial Issues than the Environment

The environment ranked last on Americans' list of issues they described as "crucial" for Congress to focus on in 2011.

Question: "Which issues are crucial, important, or not important for Congress to focus on in 2011?"

	Crucial %	Important %	Not important %	Unsure %
Jobs	72	25	2	–
The Budget Deficit	57	38	5	1
Health Care	53	41	6	–
Taxes	44	47	7	2
Afghanistan	37	46	13	3
Energy	36	53	10	1
The Environment	31	53	15	1

Taken from: Reuters/Ipsos Poll, October 28–31, 2010.

Cutting Energy Use Should Not Be Celebrated

This blindness to the vital importance of energy is precisely what Earth Hour exploits. It sends the comforting-but-false message: Cutting off fossil fuels would be easy and even fun! People spend the hour stargazing and holding torch-lit beach parties; restaurants offer special candle-lit dinners. Earth Hour makes the renunciation of energy seem like a big party.

Participants spend an enjoyable sixty minutes in the dark, safe in the knowledge that the life-saving benefits of industrial civilization are just a light switch away. This bears no relation whatsoever to what life would actually be like under the sort of draconian carbon-reduction policies that climate activists are demanding: punishing carbon taxes, severe emissions caps, outright bans on the construction of power plants.

A Life Without Energy

Forget one measly hour with just the lights off. How about Earth Month, without *any* form of fossil fuel energy? Try spending a month shivering in the dark without heating, electricity, refrigeration; without power plants or generators; without any of the labor-saving, time-saving, and therefore life-saving products that industrial energy makes possible.

Those who claim that we must cut off our carbon emissions to prevent an alleged global catastrophe need to learn the indisputable fact that cutting off our carbon emissions *would* be a global catastrophe. What we really need is greater awareness of just how indispensable carbon-based energy is to human life (including, of course, to our ability to cope with any changes in the climate).

Environmentalists Are Anti-Civilization

It is true that the importance of Earth Hour is its symbolic meaning. But that meaning is the opposite of the one intended. The lights of our cities and monuments are a symbol of human achievement, of what mankind has accomplished in rising from the cave to the skyscraper. Earth Hour presents the disturbing spectacle of people *celebrating those lights being extinguished.* Its call for people to renounce energy and to rejoice at darkened skyscrapers makes its real meaning unmistakably clear: Earth Hour symbolizes the renunciation of industrial civilization.

EVALUATING THE AUTHOR'S ARGUMENTS:

Keith Lockitch says environmentalists fail to realize how indispensable fossil fuel is to human life. How you think the other authors in this chapter would respond to this claim? Write one to two sentences per author, then state whether you agree with Lockitch on this point.

Environmentalism Is Good for Society

Lisa P. Jackson

"This isn't just about green opportunities—it's about all opportunities. The environment affects so many other critical issues."

In the following viewpoint Lisa P. Jackson argues that environmentalism has the potential to improve every sector of American society. She argues that when neighborhoods are clean and pollution free, residents are too, which keeps health care costs down. This in turn allows Americans to spend more of their money on products and services, a practice that stimulates the economy, attracts businesses, and keeps crime low. Healthy residents also go to school and work more often and are prevented from falling into cycles of drug abuse, violence, and crime. Jackson suggests that nearly every major issue facing American society—from the economy, to school performance, to health care, to urban development—is intrinsically tied to environmentalism. She concludes that environmentalism should be embraced and woven into all areas of society in order to keep America on track.

Lisa P. Jackson is head of the Environmental Protection Agency, a federal government organization charged with safeguarding America's environment.

Lisa P. Jackson, "Remarks at the National Urban League Green Jobs Summit," yosemite.epa.gov, December 2, 2009.

AS YOU READ, CONSIDER THE FOLLOWING QUESTIONS:

1. In what way are environmentalism and health care linked, according to Jackson?
2. In what way are environmental challenges linked to economic growth, according to the author?
3. Who is Mr. Green and how does he factor into Jackson's argument?

Not long ago I was at the White House with a coalition of groups for an effort called Green the Block. I was honored to be there with Dr. Dorothy Height, a woman who stood on stage with Dr. [Martin Luther] King at the March on Washington [in 1963]. I was heartened that she was there to support not just environmental justice, but economic justice. She shows us that these issues are the next step in the long march forward. This particular forum was dedicated to putting green jobs into inner city communities—based on the idea that putting environmental green on the block helps put more economic green on the block. And it was happening a few hundred feet from the Oval Office.

In a different instance, I visited West Philadelphia High School where students are working on an innovative hybrid car. The vast majority of students at West Philly—almost 100 percent—are minority. Many of them come from disadvantaged, under-served neighborhoods. The hybrid car they're building has outperformed models built by well-funded university teams and private companies with some very deep pockets. Yet, these high school students, from the inner city, are taking their car to compete against other hybrid vehicles from around the world in the Progressive Automotive X Prize competition. They've just moved to the next stage of the competition, and survived the first eliminations when more than half of the other teams were sent home. The top prize in the contest is $10 million—and they are expected to do very well.

As I said, the [Economic] Recovery Act is focused on creating green jobs. One of the signature initiatives provides funding to weatherize low-income homes all across America. That is putting thousands of people to work in their own communities. And it's benefitting the places that have the greatest need for higher employment, lower electricity bills, and cleaner air—all in one policy.

These are all great news. But the change we need is more than a few good examples and a handful of policies. When we talk about bringing green jobs to our communities, what we're really talking about is expanding the conversation we're having on environmentalism.

Environmentalism Touches Us All

For too long, environmentalism has been seen as an enclave for the privileged. Talking about the issue brings to mind sweeping vistas and wide-open landscapes. What doesn't usually come to mind is an apartment building. A city block. Or a school playground. Or, for that matter, an inner-city kid who has trouble breathing on hot days. Or a black business owner whose employees are getting sick. But we know that environmental issues are as much a part of their lives as they are for anyone.

As I just mentioned, we're using Recovery investments for home weatherization—which will create green jobs, cut emissions, and save energy. That reminds me of what one of my African American colleagues told me: the story of how, every year as winter was coming, his grandmother would get up on a chair and put up plastic sheeting over the windows. She didn't say she was "greening her home." She didn't say she was "weatherizing the house." She didn't call herself an "environmentalist." From her perspective, she was just keeping out the cold and saving money on the oil bill. But the issues that we label "environmentalism" were an important part of her life.

Today, the inauguration of the first African American president, and my confirmation as the first African American Administrator of [the Environmental Protection] Agency [EPA], has begun the process of changing the face of environmentalism in our country. We all know that's not an easy lift. Change takes work.

Environmentalism Is Linked to Opportunity

One important idea we can communicate is that this isn't just about green opportunities—it's about all opportunities. The environment affects so many other critical issues.

We can talk about our crumbling schools and how we need to rebuild them so our children can learn and get good jobs. But we have to ensure we're not building schools in the shadow of polluters that will make our kids sick, so that they miss day after day of class with asthma or other health problems.

We can talk about health care, but we also have to talk about how the poor—who get sick more often because they live in neighborhoods where the air and water are polluted—are the same people who go to the emergency room for treatment. That drives up health care costs for everyone. It hurts the local and the national economy.

We must also understand that environmental challenges in our neighborhoods hold back economic growth. Poison in the ground means poison in the economy. A weak environment means a weak consumer base. Unhealthy air means an unhealthy atmosphere for investments. And in many neighborhoods, visible environmental degradation compounds other problems.

When businesses won't invest, economic possibilities are limited. As a result crime is higher, violence is higher—often times drug use is rampant—and the vicious cycle continues. So we can talk about crime too. What have we taught young people (like my two teenage sons) to value, to aspire to, or take pride in when they see that their communities are unclean, unhealthy and unsafe—and that the people around them are unconcerned?

For those reasons and more, it's my mission at EPA to broaden this conversation—so that we can bring not just green jobs, but jobs and opportunities of every kind to the places where they are needed most.

FAST FACT

Reducing environmental risks worldwide could save 13 million lives every year, stated the World Health Organization in 2011. An analysis of health conditions in 192 countries showed that every nation is affected by environmental risks that lead to a variety of preventable health problems.

Protecting and Uplifting Communities

Let me close by telling you about someone I met recently. . . . I grew up in the upper 9th Ward [of New Orleans]. Two weeks ago, I made my first official visit as EPA Administrator to my old hometown. While I was there, I went to some of the areas hit hardest by Hurricane Katrina, including the lower 9th Ward and my old neighborhood in Pontchartrain Park.

While I was there, I met a man named Mr. Green. Mr. Green has lived in New Orleans most of his life. He's an older man, and like my

The Economic Recovery Act created thousands of green jobs in local communities throughout the country. Here, workers install energy-efficient insulation in a Columbus, Ohio, home.

mother, he lost his home and everything in it to the floods after the storm. Today, they are rebuilding on the lot where Mr. Green's house once stood.

His new home will be sustainable, energy efficient, and full of extraordinary innovative green designs and technologies. It's one of many green homes that are being built in the community—by workers from the community. And standing next to the new house is all that Mr. Green has left of his old home—the concrete steps that used to lead up to his doorway.

I had a quick moment to talk with him privately, and I asked him—"You are here as a spokesman for this green building effort. You can tell me honestly: would you call yourself an environmentalist?" He paused for a second before saying, "Well—I wasn't." But, he said, after the impact of the Hurricane, he had seen how seemingly far off issues touched his life.

He mentioned the destruction of the coastal wetlands, which had been drained or cut away for oil and gas lines before the storm. Those natural defenses against storm surges and flooding weren't there to help protect the community.

This is the kind of story I've heard often—in New Orleans and elsewhere. People who didn't think about water quality until their kids got sick. People who never thought about pollution from the local plant until the plant shut down and moved out, and no other businesses wanted to move in to the contaminated lot. People who didn't think about fuel efficiency until gas prices hit $4 a gallon.

Environmentalism Is the Future

After Hurricane Katrina, rebuilding New Orleans has focused on making the city sustainable, and tapping the potential of a growing clean energy industry. People are building efficient homes, riding hybrid buses, installing solar panels and working in green-collar jobs. Mr. Green is going to move into a new green home. The land that my old house is sitting on was recently bought by developers. They are going to turn the whole area—my old neighborhood—into a sustainable community.

This is the potential for rebuilding I see in every community. And green jobs are the key. Restoring and preserving the environment in our communities is a way to create new opportunities. It's good economic sense to make our neighborhoods healthier places to live and better places to set up a business. It's good economic sense to cut the pollution that makes employees call-in sick, or causes them to stay at home with a sick child. It's good economic sense to fix those problems by training someone in the community for a good paying job cleaning up their neighborhood.

EVALUATING THE AUTHOR'S ARGUMENTS:

Does knowing Lisa P. Jackson's position as head of the EPA influence your opinion of her argument? Does it make you more or less likely to agree with her? Explain your reasoning.

Chapter 3

What Is the State of the Environmental Movement?

Following the first Earth Day demonstrations on April 22, 1970, the environmental movement became a force in American politics.

The Environmental Movement Has Successfully Evolved

Will Marshall

"[The environmental movement has] made undeniable progress since [1970]."

In the following viewpoint Will Marshall argues that the environmental movement has successfully evolved. Over the last four decades environmentalists have cleaned up America's water and air, and have even changed the way in which contemporary environmental threats are viewed and discussed. As environmental issues have evolved, so have the methods for addressing them. The movement's major achievements of recent decades, according to Marshall, include programs that helped citizens identify health risks posed by polluters, economy-boosting ideas such as carbon pricing and cap-and-trade, and decentralizing decisions regarding the management and protection of endangered species and their habitats. Marshall says there is more work to do to clean the planet, but he concludes that the environmental movement

Will Marshall, "As the Earth Turns: How Environmentalism Has Evolved," *Huffington Post,* April 22, 2010. Reproduced by permission.

has accomplished a great deal in the forty years since the first Earth Day in 1970 and is poised to grapple with the next phase of environmental challenges.

Will Marshall is president and founder of the Progressive Policy Institute, a research and policy organization that promotes a variety of issues, including environmental legislation.

AS YOU READ, CONSIDER THE FOLLOWING QUESTIONS:

1. What is the difference between "point" and "non-point" sources of pollution, according to Marshall?
2. What is the Toxic Release Inventory, as described by Marshall?
3. What is "civic environmentalism" and how does it factor into the author's argument?

When Earth Day was first celebrated 40 years ago today [April 22, 2010], environmental distress was in our face. Rivers caught fire, oil spills fouled U.S. shores, toxic waste dumps proliferated, and Los Angeles seemed permanently wreathed in smog. Now we worry more about things we don't see—runoff and waste from farms, growing carbon concentrations in the atmosphere, fish disappearing from the oceans.

Much Progress Has Been Made

This change underscores both the successes and the limits of the "first generation" of environmental law and regulation. Starting with the landmark Clean Air Act of 1970, Americans for the first time began to grapple seriously with the environmental havoc wrought by the industrial revolution.

We've made undeniable progress since then, as [*New Republic* contributing editor] Gregg Easterbrook and other writers have documented. Our air and water are cleaner. This would be a good day, in fact, for environmentalists and their business antagonists not to indulge in the usual doomsday talk. What we've learned since the first Earth Day is that ecological calamity isn't inevitable, that the damage we do to nature is often reversible, and that we can curb pollution without wrecking our economy.

More Needs to Be Done

Republicans still cling to the myth that a clean environment is a luxury we can't afford, hence their refusal to take climate change seriously. And some environmental activists evidently believe that alarmism in the defense of ecological health is no vice. If the idea is to shake Americans out of their "denial" about global warming, the opposite seems to be happening. Polls show the public is growing more skeptical about the hazards of climate change. Allegations (unfounded, as it turns out) that British university researchers cooked climate data in an excess of environmental correctness haven't helped.

Firemen extinguish a fire on a bridge caused by the burning Ohio River in 1969. This was among one of the environmental disasters that led to the formation of the environmental movement.

Even discounting for some hyperbole, however, the new environmental challenges are real enough. Unlike the great industrial cleanup, which focused on specific "point sources" of pollution like smokestacks and drainage pipes, we're faced today with damage from "non-point" sources like fields and hog farms, high-tech fishing fleets and the millions of cars, dry cleaners, lawnmowers and even cows pumping carbon and other greenhouse gases into the atmosphere.

The top-down, "command and control" regulations of the first generation of environment activism could not cope effectively with these new problems. That's why PPI [Progressive Policy Institute] back in the 1990s started advocating a "second generation" of policy tools for dealing with new and more diffuse ecological challenges. Examples include innovations like the Toxic Release Inventory, which allows citizens to find out about health risks posed by local polluters; market incentives like carbon pricing and the cap-and-trade system first set up in 1990 to combat acid rain; and "civic environmentalism," which decentralizes decisions about, say, how to manage habitat vital to endangered species, from Washington regulators to local landowners.

Fast Fact

A 2011 annual report by the American Lung Association found that more than half of the most smog-polluted cities in the United States reported a decrease in smog levels. In addition, twenty-three of the twenty-five most polluted cities had improved since the previous year's report, and nineteen cities had reported their best particle pollution levels ever.

Next Wave of Environmentalism

Now it appears as though we're heading into a third phase, in which environmental and energy policy merge into one. The environmental movement traditionally has aimed at mitigating the impact of industrial society on nature. Now we're talking about something truly revolutionary—a shift from a dirty economy powered by cheap fossil fuels to a clean, low-carbon economy. This prospect beckons not only because of the environmental benefits, which would be large, but also

The Environmental Movement Has Done More Good than Harm

The majority of Americans think that the environmental movement has probably or definitely done more good than harm, according to a recurring poll conducted by Gallup. However, the percentage of Americans who hold such positive views of the movement has fallen over the last two decades, indicating decreasing satisfaction with the movement's overall performance.

Question: "Would you say the environmental movement in this nation has done definitely more good than harm, probably more good than harm, probably more harm than good, or definitely more harm than good?"

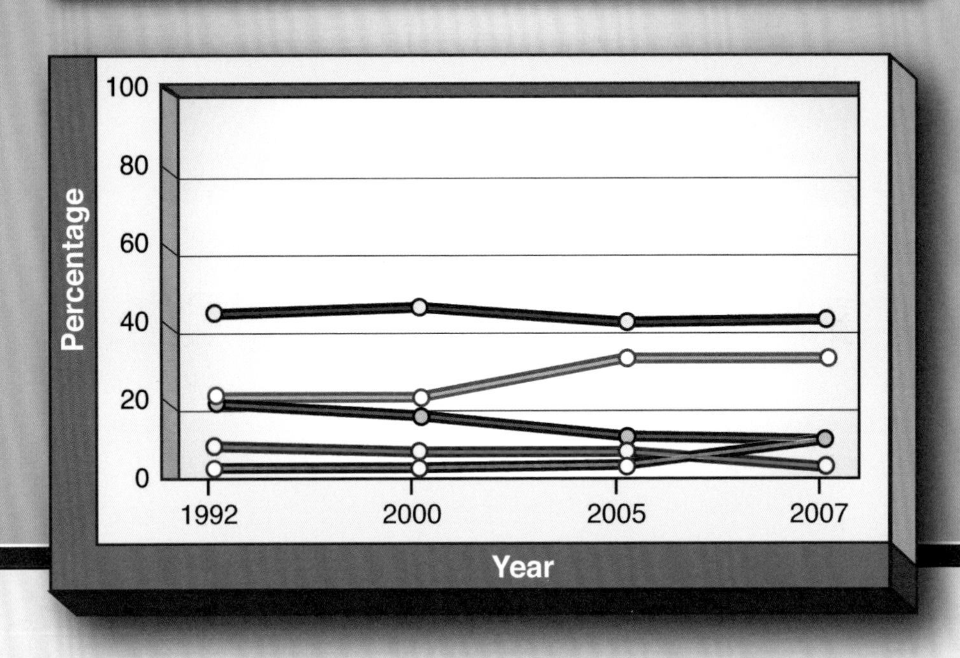

Taken from: Gallup Poll. March 11–14, 2007.

because of the potential for immense economic and security gains. It would enable the United States to reduce its costly dependence on foreign oil suppliers, many of whom don't have our best interests at heart. And it opens up broad new avenues for economic innovation and growth in the development of clean technology and fuels.

Some will use Earth Day to depict America as an energy wastrel and despoiler of the earth. Instead of donning hair shirts, progressives ought to stress America's opportunity to lead the world toward its clean energy future.

EVALUATING THE AUTHOR'S ARGUMENTS:

Will Marshall uses facts, statistics, examples, and reasoning to make his argument that the environmental movement has been a success. He does not, however, use any quotations to support his points. If you were to rewrite this article and insert quotations, what authorities might you quote from? Where would you place quotations, and why?

The Environmental Movement Is Dead

Gregory Vickrey

In the following viewpoint Gregory Vickrey argues that the environmental movement has sold out, succumbing to corporate influence, and is dead. In his opinion, environmental organizations are more interested in making money than they are in saving the planet. He accuses several such organizations of partnering with the very corporations that pollute the planet, which in Vickrey's opinion proves environmental organizations are hypocritical and disingenuous. He also accuses many high-profile environmentalists, such as former vice president Al Gore and Senators John Kerry and Joe Lieberman, of having conflicted connections to companies that exploit nature or otherwise act unscrupulously. For all of these reasons Vickrey concludes that the environmental movement has become just another special interest group devoted more to dollars than to saving the planet.

Gregory Vickrey is a consultant to nonprofit organizations.

"Environmentalism is dead."

Gregory Vickrey, "Environmentalism Is Dead," CounterPunch.org, May 21–23, 2010. Reproduced by permission.

AS YOU READ, CONSIDER THE FOLLOWING QUESTIONS:

1. List at least five of the Nature Conservancy's corporate partners, as reported by Vickrey.
2. In the author's opinion, what is incongruent about Al Gore's involvement with the Alliance for Climate Protection and his role at Apple Computers?
3. What does Vickrey mean when he says environmental organizations are more interested in seven figures than the next seven generations?

Another tragedy befalls the environment and we can count on those that were once environmentalists to capitalize, figuratively and literally. As you read, perhaps 1000 or so organizations are happily signing (or being bribed to sign) yet another refined letter to President [Barack] Obama, praising his efforts to date and encouraging 'change'. With stellar coordination, you witness the appeals via email from these faux-enviros that clearly state how you can save the sea turtles, or protect the shrimp, or rid us of our reliance on oil by donating today.

Faux Environmentalism Abounds

This particular letter in circulation is about climate change, and is directly tied to the Gulf of Mexico in its appeal. As it stands, responsibility for pushing the letter lies with the minions at The Nature Conservancy (TNC), National Wildlife Federation (NWF), Repower America aka the Climate Protection Action Fund aka The Alliance For Climate Protection (RA), and a few others.

The letter begins with 'applause', as one would expect. Continue reading, and, apparently, President Obama has done an amazing job prioritizing clean energy, solving the climate crisis, enacting fuel efficiency standards that are defining a new paradigm for vehicular motion, and hitting all the right buttons at the Environmental Protection Agency. Who knew?

One can naturally assume The Nature Conservancy, National Wildlife Federation, and Repower America know. And with a thousand or so other signatures on yet another letter driven by the same old set of corporate enviros, the rest of us know something as well.

Environmentalism is dead.

The Nature Conservancy receives a corporate check from a Kraft Foods Crystal Light executive at a fundraiser. Critics say corporate involvement has hijacked the environmental movement.

Environmentalism Has Sold Out

In its place we have the notions of 'pragmatic solutions' and 'non-controversial approaches' to appreciate.

Such words of discourse come from The Nature Conservancy itself. It is a disgrace to ecosystems everywhere and the next seven generations that they pimp nature dot org as their official website. A quick look-see into the world of TNC and comprehension dawns. Their corporate partners in environmental crime and shame:

3M Company
Alliant Energy
Altria Group
American Electric Power
Bank of America
Barrick Gold Corporation
The Boeing Company
BP
Cargill
Caterpillar Inc.
Chevron
The Coca-Cola Company
Delta Air Lines
The Dow Chemical Company
Duke Energy Corporation
Eastman Kodak Company
Ecolab Inc.
ExxonMobil Corporation
MeadWestvaco Corporation
Monsanto Company
Nestlé Waters North America
PG&E Corporation
Plum Creek Timber Company
SC Johnson & Son, Inc.
Temple-Inland
Weyerhaeuser Company
Xerox Corporation

Scratching your temple?

It is difficult to tell which organization was the most influential in writing the letter to President Obama, but it reads with the gimmickry of a [Bush political adviser] Karl Rove production. Examining information about the National Wildlife Federation makes one consider that they, NWF, may have been the lead, considering they take donations from the likes of the US Environmental Protection Agency, the US Department of Defense, The Boeing Company, Walt Disney Company, and on, and on, and on. Care to visit with a [Bush deputy secretary of defense Paul] Wolfowitz at a fundraiser? Throw a few thousand at NWF.

The mathematics of connection get simpler, even as the names get more complicated, with Repower America aka blah blah and blah. The CEO of National Wildlife Federation is on the board at RA. Repower America prostitutes itself with absurdity while dancing with [Senators] John Kerry, Joe Lieberman, and Lindsey Graham—the "authors" of some pile of papers related to some charade about some climate (shout out to NRDC [Natural Resources Defense Council]!) that will serve no useful purpose other than to keep the timber industry viable. Seeking relevance, [former vice president and environmentalist] Al Gore may be seen here at RA when he is not serving in his role at Apple Computer, Inc. of child-labor/sweatshop city fame. Repower America is also blessed with the presence of Joseph Stiglitz, a former Vice President at that most prestigious of entities, the World Bank.

To quote a Wonder Pet, "This. Is. Serious."

Environmentalism Is Dead

Environmentalism is dead. It has been co-opted and corrupted to the point of absolute strangulation, and what remains of the corpse is being devoured rapaciously by the necrophiliacs at your favorite corporate-controlled big enviro—yes, the list of cannibals is much longer than The Nature Conservancy, National Wildlife Federation, and Repower America, and the responsibility lies with those not herein named to prove themselves worthy candidates for resurrection as organizations willing to serve the next seven generations instead of the next seven figures.

Without environmentalism, there are no environmentalists.

We must save ourselves and our planet as humans.

EVALUATING THE AUTHOR'S ARGUMENTS:

Gregory Vickrey accuses environmental groups such as the National Wildlife Federation, Repower America, the Nature Conservancy, and other groups of being unresponsive to and even profiting from environmental distress. Pick one of these groups and research its environmental programs and partnerships. Read reviews and critiques of its work. Then, write a five-paragraph essay in which you report what you learned and state whether you agree with Vickrey's allegations.

The Environmental Movement Promotes Terrorism

Rich Trzupek

"[Environmental terrorist James Jay Lee] is hardly the only example of someone taking the Green movement's message to its logical and extreme conclusions."

In the following viewpoint Rich Trzupek argues that the environmental movement uses illegal, violent, even terrorist tactics. He explains that all environmentalists share the same goal: the protection of animals, habitat, and the planet. This makes them inherently anti-human, in Trzupek's opinion. He offers examples of groups and individuals who have committed violent and illegal acts in their pursuit of environmentalism. Trzupek says that because environmentalist rhetoric is so hysterical and inflated, it naturally incites unstable people to commit violence, even if moderate environmentalists would not commit violence themselves. Trzupek concludes that environmentalists seek the destruction of human civilization and should therefore be considered a terrorist group.

Rich Trzupek is a chemist and a writer whose columns have appeared in the *Chicago Tribune* and *FrontPage Magazine.*

AS YOU READ, CONSIDER THE FOLLOWING QUESTIONS:

1. What is the Voluntary Human Extinction Movement as described by the author?
2. What does the term "monkeywrenching" mean as used by Trzupek?
3. How does Trzupek say James Jay Lee interpreted the environmentalist value of protecting against overpopulation?

There's no doubt that Discovery Channel gunman James Jay Lee[1] was mentally unstable, but it should be equally clear that Lee is far from the first person—and surely not the last—to take their cues from an environmental movement that grows more delusional with each passing day. Does that mean that we should blame [former vice president and environmentalist] Al Gore for Lee's actions and death? No. Gore is far too savvy a huckster to endanger the green gold-mine that he helped create by encouraging violence among his followers. He would much prefer that the James Jay Lees of the world save the planet by making a substantial purchase of carbon credits on the CCX [Chicago Climate Exchange]. That said, Gore, the Sierra Club, Greenpeace, and all the rest of today's self-proclaimed environmental champions surely share the blame for creating the atmosphere of fear and dread that permeates America's attitude about our relationship with nature. It is the misguided notion that human beings are an infection on planet Earth, a feeling shared by millions of Americans, that provided James Jay Lee with an outlet for his paranoid delusions, just as it did for [Unabomber] Ted Kaczynski thirty years ago.

Extreme and Unreasonable

Environmental advocates have continually upped the ante when it comes to doomsday rhetoric, to the point that they are now "all in" [i.e., have played all their "chips"]. They have progressed from the bird extinction delusions that Rachel Carson chronicled in *Silent Spring*[2] to a crisis they claim is so acute, so immediate, that all forms of life on earth are in grave danger. Is it any wonder that some people

1. On September 1, 2010, Lee took hostages at the Discovery Channel's offices in Silver Spring, Maryland.
2. The 1962 book that helped launch the environmental movement.

might take them at their word and act accordingly? A mentally unstable man like James Jay Lee wielding a bomb might grab the spotlight for a few days, but he is hardly the only example of someone taking the Green movement's message to its logical and extreme conclusions.

Consider the Voluntary Human Extinction Movement for example. Proudly proclaiming "may we all live long and die out," VHEMT says that "phasing out the human race by voluntarily ceasing to breed will allow Earth's biosphere to return to good health. Crowded conditions and resource shortages will improve as we become less dense." Members aren't inclined to hasten the process along by blowing fellow human beings up, but their goal is indistinguishable from James Jay Lee's: once humans stop procreating, the world returns to pristine purity. Less subtly, the Church of Euthanasia asks visitors to "Save the Planet: Kill Yourself" and instructs followers to abide by its "four pillars" of faith: suicide, abortion, cannibalism and sodomy. Are these two extreme examples? Sure, but theirs are hardly isolated points of view. A James Jay Lee would feel right at home commiserating with like-minded souls who belong to organizations like VHEMT or the Church of Euthanasia. Such organizations may have counseled Lee against violent means, but they surely would have sympathized with his ends.

Fast Fact

In 2008 the FBI reported that its counterterrorism agents had conducted investigations of over two thousand ecocrimes since 1979, with an estimated loss of over $110 million to a range of victims, from lumber companies to international corporations to animal-testing facilities to genetic-research firms.

Using Illegal Tactics and Violence

The Earth First! movement proudly proclaims that it's growing in size and importance. The radical organization urges people concerned with the fate of the planet to use any tactic, legal or illegal, to save the planet. *The Earth First! Journal* describes their mission thus: "Earth First! formed in 1979, in response to an increasingly corporate, compromising and ineffective environmental community. It is not an organization, but a movement. There are no "members" of EF!, only Earth First!ers. We believe in using all of the tools in the toolbox, from grassroots and legal organizing to civil disobedience and monkeywrenching. When the law won't fix the problem, we put our bodies on the line to stop the destruction." The term "monkeywrenching" is of course code that covers a variety of offenses, from spiking trees to burning down subdivisions, all in the name of making the earth a better place in which to live.

At first blush it may seem ironic that radical groups and ideas like these could sprout up in a nation that has made such incredible strides in cleaning up the environment over the last forty years. Yet, upon closer inspection, it makes sense. America has dedicated billions and billions of dollars in both the public and private sector toward environmental protection and restoration. Congress has passed law after law that requires cleaner air, water and soil. No matter. The tenor and substance of the message [from] people like Al Gore and organizations like the Sierra Club has not changed, no matter how much time and money we invest and how much progress me make. In fact, they never admit that we have made any progress all. In this circumstance, a committed environmentalist can only conclude that government is incapable of fixing the problem, either because politicians are incompetent, or because corporations are too powerful, or both. The people that ardent environmentalists trust—like Gore and the Sierra Club—assure them that the planet is in worse danger than ever today. Government solutions have failed. So what's left? Clearly, for folks like those represented by VHEMT, the Church of Euthanasia and Earth First! radical solutions are the only thing left. Nothing else has worked.

Attacking Humans to Save Animals

James Jay Lee is an extreme example of an illness that permeates American culture. While "mainstream" environmentalists and environmental groups may not condone his methods or his words, most are wholly committed to his goals. Environmentalists worry about over-population and civilization encroaching on wildlife habitats. James Jay Lee translated that into: "Saving the Planet means saving

Ecoterrorist Attacks Have Become More Frequent

Although most ecoterrorist attacks cause less than $10,000 in damages, they have increased in frequency.

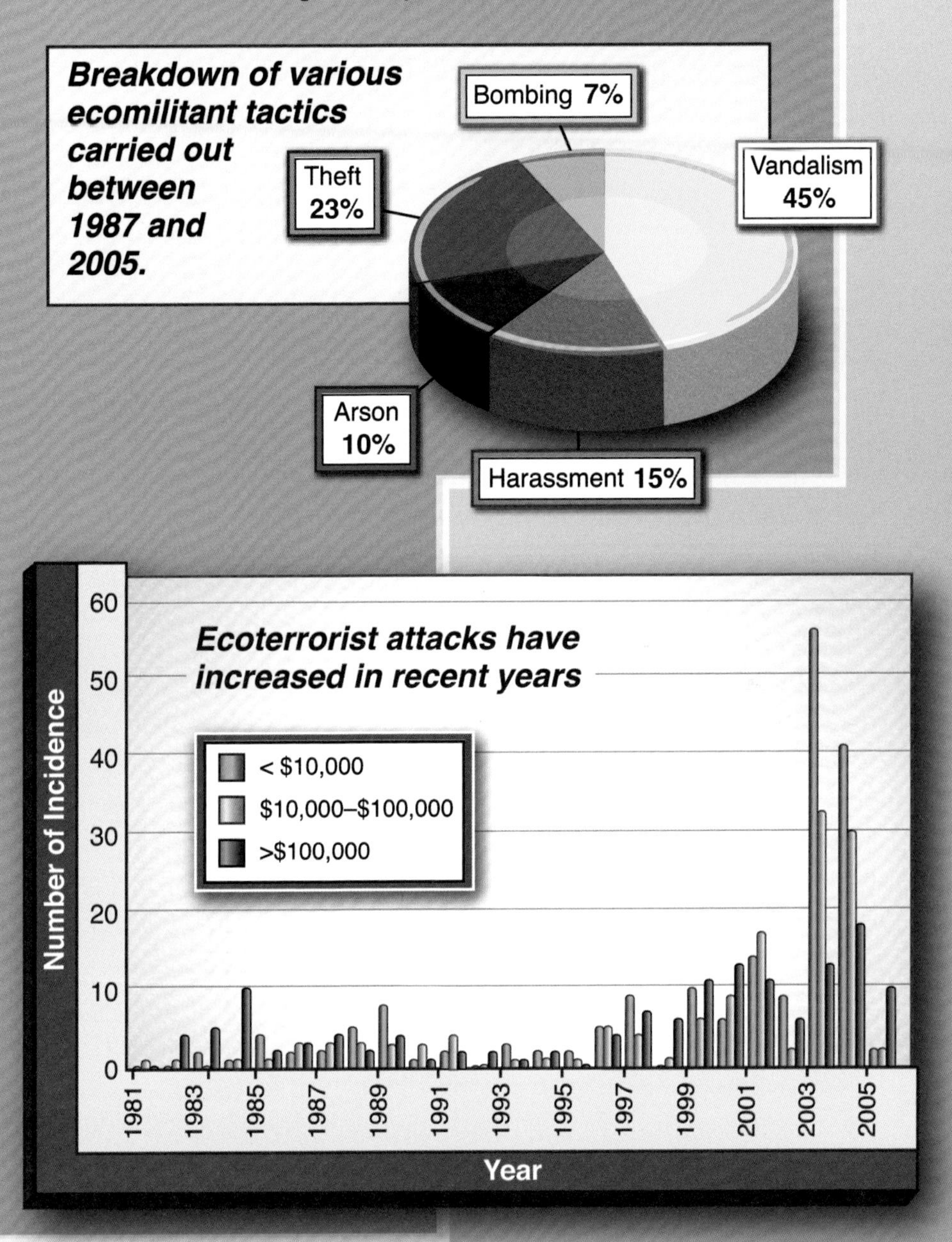

Taken from: Department of Homeland Security, "Ecotourism: Environmental and Animal-Rights Militants in the United States."

what's left of the non-human Wildlife by decreasing the Human population. That means stopping the human race from breeding any more disgusting human babies!" Environmentalists wag their fingers and lecture that humans are responsible for pollution and so we must do more to clean up this dirty planet. James Jay Lee expressed that idea more succinctly: "Humans are the most destructive, filthy, pollutive creatures around and are wrecking what's left of the planet. . . ." Environmentalists wring their hands about endangered species and supposedly endangered species (like polar bears). James Jay Lee took that message to heart: "Nothing is more important than saving them. The Lions, Tigers, Giraffes, Elephants, Froggies, Turtles, Apes, Raccoons, Beetles, Ants, Sharks, Bears, and of course the Squirrels."

Environmental apologists on the left have attempted to condemn any attempt to link Lee to their movement, claiming that doing so exposes the hypocrisy of conservatives who complain about attempts to link violence and racism to the tea party movement [a political movement that gained momentum in 2010]. These two examples bear no practical resemblance to each other. The tea party movement's focus is overwhelmingly on making a difference by working legally within our system of government. To wit: by exercising the movement's power at the ballot box. The environmental movement has continually sent its followers the message that government has not and, by inference, cannot solve the global ecological "crisis". Additionally, while there are incidents of politically motivated violence on the right, it would be very surprising to learn that such incidents outnumber those involving leftist-inspired violence. In the case of political causes, in other words, both sides are equally infected by extremists. But, when it comes to the environment, however, extremism and violence is a one way affair. There is no group analogous to Earth First!, VHEMT or the Church of Euthanasia on the skeptical side of the environmental movement. There is no one analogous to James Jay Lee or Ted Kaczynski. The strongest voices aligned against green extremists are lawful, non-violent think tanks like the Cato Institute and the Heartland Institute. While organizations like Heartland receive death threats from time to time, they don't issue them and, more important, nothing they say or do would inspire

James Jay Lee protests in front of Discovery Channel headquarters in 2008. On September 1, 2010, he took hostages at the headquarters and was shot and killed by police.

their followers to believe that such violent measures are necessary. Environmental groups can't come close to making the same claims after decades of overblown hyperbole and scare-mongering. Al Gore and his cohorts, in other words, may not have pushed James Jay Lee over the edge, but there is no way that troubled man would have gotten close to his particular precipice but for Gore and his disciples.

EVALUATING THE AUTHOR'S ARGUMENTS:

Rich Trzupek uses extreme examples of environmentalists and environmental groups to make his argument that all environmental values logically lead toward violent, anti-human ends. Do you agree with him? Do you think it is fair of him to only offer examples of extremist environmental groups? Why or why not? In your opinion, do all environmental groups approve of the tactics Trzupek discusses? Support your answer with specific examples.

Environmentalists Have Been Unfairly Labeled as Terrorists

"Labeling activists as terrorists wastes valuable anti-terrorism resources and is an insult to everyone who died [on 9/11]."

Will Potter

In the following viewpoint Will Potter argues that environmentalists have been wrongly branded as terrorists. In truth, he says, environmentalists are just activists who lawfully exercise their rights to free speech and assembly. Potter explains that environmentalists threaten corporate profits when they boycott companies that test on animals, encourage people to drive less, and avoid meat and other animal products. Potter thinks that, because they challenge American culture, environmentalists have become the target of a government campaign of harassment and intimidation. Potter admits that some environmentalists break the law in pursuit of their beliefs. But the vast majority are lawful people who engage in nonviolent civil disobedience, he says. Potter concludes that environmentalists are victims of a mass targeting campaign by the government simply because their beliefs are radical and unpopular.

Will Potter, "What Is the 'Green Scare'?," Greenisthenewred.com, September 1, 2008. Reproduced by permission.

Will Potter is a journalist and the author of the book *Green Is The New Red: An Insider's Account of a Social Movement Under Siege.* He runs a blog that explores the ways in which animal rights and environmental activists have been labeled ecoterrorists.

AS YOU READ, CONSIDER THE FOLLOWING QUESTIONS:

1. What is the "Green Scare," as described by the author?
2. What is *Hoot* and why was it labeled ecoterrorism, according to Potter?
3. In what way do the environmental and animal rights movements threaten corporate profits, according to the author?

"The No. 1 domestic terrorism threat," says John Lewis, a top FBI official, "is the eco-terrorism, animal-rights movement."

The animal rights and environmental movements, like every other social movement throughout history, have both legal and illegal elements. There are people who leaflet, write letters, and lobby. There are people who protest and engage in non-violent civil disobedience. And there are people, like the Animal Liberation Front and Earth Liberation Front, who go out at night with black masks and break windows, burn SUVs, and release animals from fur farms.

The Green Scare

Animal rights and environmental advocates have not flown planes into buildings, taken hostages, or sent Anthrax through the mail. They have never even injured anyone. In fact, the only act of attempted murder in the history of the U.S. animal rights movement was coordinated by corporate provocateurs. Yet the FBI ranks these activists as the top domestic terrorism threat. And the Department of Homeland Security lists them on its roster of national security threats, while ignoring right-wing extremists who have bombed the Oklahoma City federal building, murdered doctors, and admittedly created weapons of mass destruction.

This disproportionate, heavy-handed government crackdown on the animal rights and environmental movements, and the reckless use of the word "terrorism," is often called the Green Scare.

Much like the Red Scare and the communist witch hunts of the 40s and 50s, the Green Scare is using one word—this time, it's "terrorist"—to push a political agenda, instill fear, and chill dissent. And much like the Red Scare, the Green Scare is operating on three levels: legal, legislative, and what we'll call extra-legal, or scare-mongering.

An Unfair "Eco-Terrorist" Act

The courts are being used to push conventional boundaries of what constitutes "terrorism" and to hit non-violent activists with disproportionate sentences. . . .

Even with these sweeping, and successful, legal attacks on activists, corporations and the politicians who represent them want even more power.

With just six members of Congress in the room, just hours after lawmakers and celebrities were on hand to break ground for the new memorial honoring that terrorist Martin Luther King Jr. [MLK], the House of Representatives passed the [2006] Animal Enterprise Terrorism Act [AETA], a law so vague and broad that the non-violent tactics of MLK and [Mohandas] Gandhi are now "terrorism." The bill expanded the Animal Enterprise Protection Act, the law used to convict the SHAC 7[1] of "animal enterprise terrorism" just months earlier. In true Orwellian[2] doublespeak, proponents said the law couldn't be used to convict so-called extremists, and must be expanded.

Even after the federal law passed, corporations still want more. There's been a push for state "eco-terrorism" legislation similar to the federal AETA, including the California Animal Enterprise Protection Act.

Fast Fact

The FBI lists as its top ten most wanted terrorists the following people: Osama bin Laden (now deceased), Adam Yahiye Gadahn, Daniel Andreas San Diego, Ayman al-Zawahiri, Fahd Mohammed Ahmed al-Quso, Jamel Ahmed Mohammed Ali al-Badawi, Mohammed Ali Hamadei, Ali Atwa, Hasan Izz-al-Din, and Abdullah Ahmed Abdullah. Only one of these, San Diego, is associated with environmental terrorism.

1. An animal rights group that ran a controversial website advocating legal and illegal activity to protest an animal testing lab.
2. A reference to George Orwell's dystopian novel *1984*.

FBI official John Lewis caused controversy by stating that the major domestic terrorism threat is from ecoterrorism and the animal rights movement. He was criticized for ignoring the domestic threat posed by right-wing militia groups.

Relentless Scare-Mongering

Perhaps the most dangerous wing of this Green Scare is the relentless scare-mongering.

- *Ad Campaigns.* The new McCarthyists[3] have used their deep pocketbooks and PR [public relations] savvy to place a terrorist in every shadow. They've taken out full-page anonymous ads in both *The New York Times* and *The Washington Post* labeling animal rights activists as "terrorists" for being a little too successful, and knocking a controversial animal testing laboratory from the New York Stock Exchange.
- *Public Relations Campaigns.* Not even children's movies are safe from the relentless green baiting and guilt by association. Industry groups labeled *Hoot*, a bestselling book and popular movie, "soft-

3. A reference to Senator Joseph McCarthy, who in the 1950s led an aggressive and unscrupulous effort to ferret out US members of the Communist Party.

core eco-terrorism" because the teenage protagonists try to save an endangered owl from developers. Apparently even [children's author] E.B. White was an "eco-terrorist": According to the Center for Consumer Freedom, the movie remake of [children's book and film] *Charlotte's Web* promotes animal rights extremism.

- *Surveillance, Harassment and Infiltration.* The corporate and government scare-mongering has been used to create a political climate that justifies surveillance and harassment of political advocates. For instance, the FBI is looking for informants to infiltrate vegan potlucks, Joint Terrorism Task Forces are spying on HoneyBaked Ham protestors, and corporations are tracking who activists are dating. . . .

Activists Targeted Because They Threaten Profits

The government and corporations haven't tried to hide the fact that this is all meant to protect corporate profits. The Department of Homeland Security, in a bulletin to law enforcement agencies, warned: "Attacks against corporations by animal rights extremists and eco-terrorists are costly to the targeted company and, over time, can undermine confidence in the economy."

And in a leaked PowerPoint presentation given by the State Department to corporations, we learn: "Although incidents related to terrorism are most likely to make the front-page news, animal rights extremism is what's most likely to affect your day-to-day business operations."

Underground activists like the Animal Liberation Front and Earth Liberation Front directly threaten corporate profits by doing things like burning bulldozers or sabotaging animal research equipment. But they're not the only ones.

The entire animal rights and environmental movements, perhaps more than any other social movements, directly threaten corporate profits. They do it every day. Every time activists encourage people to go vegan, every time they encourage people to stop driving, every time they encourage people to consume fewer resources and live simply. Those boycotts are permanent, and these industries know it. In many ways, the Green Scare, like the Red Scare, can be seen as a culture war, a war of values. . . .

Most Environmentalists Are Not Terrorists

Environmentalists are responsible for very few of the terrorist attacks that occur each year. Of the 75,294 terrorist attacks that occurred worldwide in 2010, just 14 were committed by environmentalists.

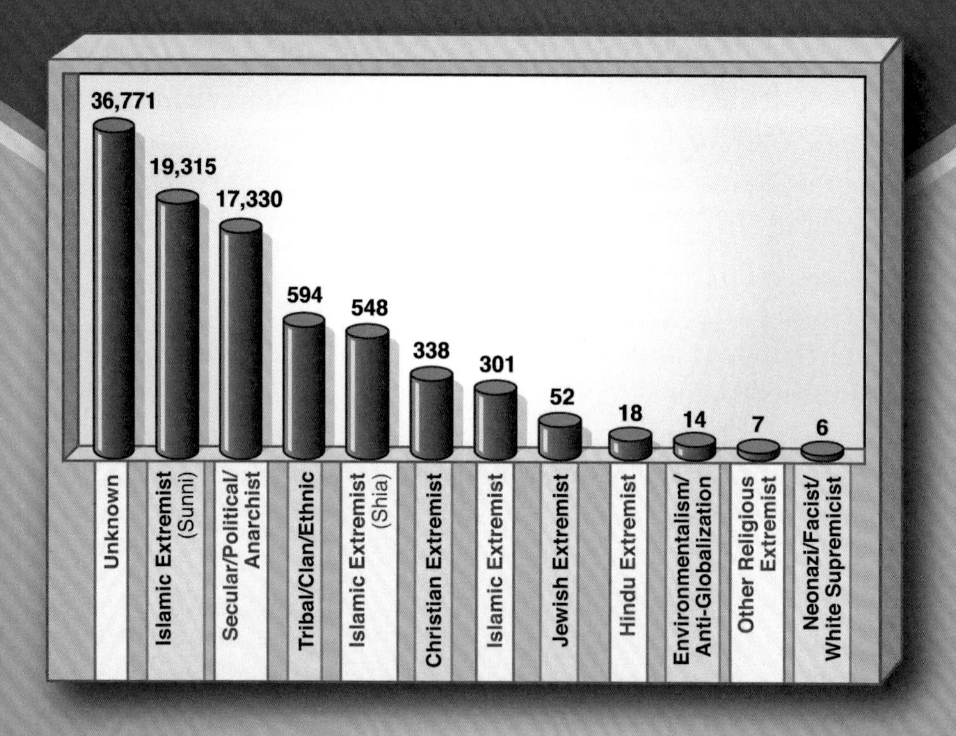

Taken from: Worldwide Incidents Tracking System, National Counterterrorism Center, March 4, 2011.

It Is All About Fear

Fear. It's all about fear. The point is to protect corporate profits by instilling fear in the mainstream animal rights and environmental movements—and every other social movement paying attention—and make people think twice about using their First Amendment rights.

Industry groups say "this is just the starting gun" for the Green Scare. But this could be the starting gun for activists as well. I've talked with hundreds of activists around the country over the years. There's a lot of fear. But there's also a lot of rage. And that's a very good thing.

Today's repression may mimic many of the tactics of the Red Scare, but today's response cannot. It's not enough to cowardly distance ourselves from anyone branded a communist, I mean, terrorist. Naming names and making loyalty oaths didn't protect activists then, and it won't protect activists now.

The only way activists, and the First Amendment, are going to get through this is by coming out and confronting it head-on. That means reaching out to mainstream Americans and telling them that labeling activists as terrorists wastes valuable anti-terrorism resources and is an insult to everyone who died in the Twin Towers [on September 11, 2001]. That means reaching out to other activists and saying loud and clear that these activists are just the canaries in the mine.

Together, we can stop the cycle of history repeating itself.

EVALUATING THE AUTHOR'S ARGUMENTS:

Will Potter admits that some animal rights and environmental activists break the law. Some smash windows, release animals from labs, set vehicles on fire, and perform other acts of vandalism in pursuit of their beliefs. Do you think the government should treat these activities as terrorism? Why or why not? In your opinion, what constitutes an act of terrorism? Use examples and quotes from the texts you have read in your answer.

The Environmental Movement Has Become Trendy and Superficial

"Stop searching online for recycled gift wrapping paper and sustainably farmed Christmas trees. Go beyond green fads for a month, and instead help make green history."

Mike Tidwell

Mike Tidwell is the executive director of the Chesapeake Climate Action Network. In the following viewpoint he argues that the environmental movement largely comprises small, superficial, even silly gestures that do not effect real environmental change. Rather than planning green weddings, buying organic napkins, or using recyclable grocery bags, Tidwell says solutions to today's environmental problems will come from large-scale political action that will reduce America's dependence on fossil fuels and develop alternative energy sources. Tidwell suggests that the green movement has become a pop culture fad represented by superficial gestures. These gestures have distracted Americans and lulled them into thinking they are taking important action toward reducing climate change when in actuality they are wasting time. Tidwell

Mike Tidwell, "To Fix Climate Change, Stop Going Green All Alone," *Washington Post,* December 6, 2009. Reprinted with permission.

urges all Americans to forgo small environmental gestures and engage in meaningful large-scale political action instead.

AS YOU READ, CONSIDER THE FOLLOWING QUESTIONS:

1. What does Tidwell say is the difference between green gestures and green political action?
2. What percentage of household lightbulbs does the author say are compact fluorescents?
3. What would be more helpful to the planet, according to Tidwell, than spending the day caulking one's windows?

As President [Barack] Obama heads to Copenhagen next week [December 2009] for global warming talks, there's one simple step Americans back home can take to help out: Stop "going green." Just stop it. No more compact fluorescent light bulbs. No more green wedding planning. No more organic toothpicks for holiday hors d'oeuvres.

Small Actions Are Meaningless

December should be national Green-Free Month. Instead of continuing our faddish and counterproductive emphasis on small, voluntary actions, we should follow the example of Americans during past moral crises and work toward large-scale change. The country's last real moral and social revolution was set in motion by the civil rights movement. And in the 1960s, civil rights activists didn't ask bigoted Southern governors and sheriffs to consider "10 Ways to Go Integrated" at their convenience.

Green gestures we have in abundance in America. Green political action, not so much. And the gestures ("Look honey, another *Vanity Fair* Green Issue!") lure us into believing that broad change is happening when the data shows that it isn't. Despite all our talk about washing clothes in cold water, we aren't making much of a difference.

For eight years, [former president] George W. Bush promoted voluntary action as the nation's primary response to global warming—and for eight years, aggregate greenhouse gas emissions remained unchanged. Even today, only 10 percent of our household light bulbs are compact fluorescents. Hybrids account for only 2.5 percent of U.S. auto sales. One can almost imagine the big energy companies secretly applauding each time we distract ourselves from the big picture with a hectoring list of "5 Easy Ways to Green Your Office."

Large-Scale Green Action Is Needed

As America joins the rest of the world in finally fighting global warming, we need to bring our battle plan up to scale. If you believe that astronauts have been to the moon and that the world is not flat, then you probably believe the satellite photos showing the Greenland ice sheet in full-on meltdown. Much of Manhattan and the Eastern Shore of Maryland may join the Atlantic Ocean in our lifetimes. Entire Pacific island nations will disappear. Hurricanes will bring untold destruction. Rising sea levels and crippling droughts will decimate crops and cause widespread famine. People will go hungry, and people will die.

Morally, this is sort of a big deal. It would be wrong to let all this happen when we have the power to prevent the worst of it by adopting clean-energy policies.

Fast Fact

A poll conducted in El Paso, Texas, by the Reuel Group discovered that just under 30 percent of respondents support a ban on plastic shopping bags, while 48.1 percent did not want plastic bags banned, and another 20.2 percent said consumers should have a choice between plastic and paper.

But how do we do that? Again, look to the history of the civil rights struggle. After many decades of public denial and inaction, the civil rights movement helped Americans to see Southern apartheid in moral terms. From there, the movement succeeded by working toward legal change. Segregation was phased out rapidly only because it was phased out through the law. These statutes didn't erase racial prejudice from every American heart overnight. But through them, our country made staggering progress. Just consider who occupies the White House today.

All who appreciate the enormity of the climate crisis still have a responsibility to make every change possible in their personal lives. I

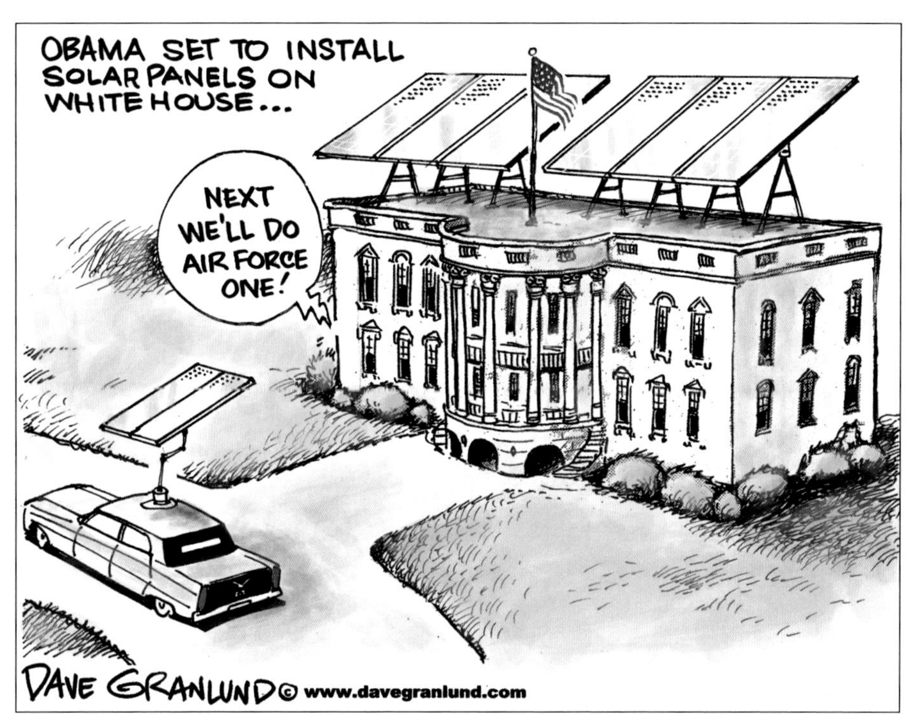

© 2010 Dave Granlund, PoliticalCartoons.com.

have, from the solar panels on my roof to the Prius in my driveway to my low-carbon-footprint vegetarian diet. But surveys show that very few people are willing to make significant voluntary changes, and those of us who do create the false impression of mass progress as the media hypes our actions.

Instead, most people want carbon reductions to be mandated by laws that will allow us to share both the responsibilities and the benefits of change. Ours is a nation of laws; if we want to alter our practices in a deep and lasting way, this is where we must start. After years of delay and denial and green half-measures, we must legislate a stop to the burning of coal, oil and natural gas.

Of course, all this will require congressional action, and therein lies the source of Obama's Copenhagen headache. To have been in the strongest position to negotiate a binding emissions treaty with other world leaders this month, the president needed a strong carbon-cap bill out of Congress. But the House of Representatives passed only a weak bill riddled with loopholes in June, and the Senate has failed to get even that far.

The "Go Green" Movement Has Supplanted Real Action

So what's the problem? There's lots of blame to go around, but the distraction of the "go green" movement has played a significant role. Taking their cues from the popular media and cautious politicians, many Americans have come to believe that they are personally to blame for global warming and that they must fix it, one by one, at home. And so they either do as they're told—a little of this, a little of that—or they feel overwhelmed and do nothing.

We all got into this mess together. And now, with treaty talks under way internationally and Congress stalled at home, we need to act accordingly. Don't spend an hour changing your light bulbs. Don't take a day to caulk your windows. Instead, pick up a phone, open a laptop, or travel to a U.S. Senate office near you and turn the tables: "What are the 10 green statutes you're working on to save the planet, Senator?"

Demand a carbon-cap bill that mandates the number 350. That's the level of carbon pollution scientists say we must limit ourselves to: 350 parts per million of CO_2 in the air. If we can stabilize the atmosphere at that number in coming decades, we should be able to avoid the worst-case scenario and preserve a planet similar to the one human civilization developed on. To get there, America will need to make deep but achievable pollution cuts well before 2020. And to protect against energy price shocks during this transition, Congress must include a system of direct rebates to consumers, paid for by auctioning permit fees to the dirty-energy companies that continue to pollute our sky.

Obama, too, needs to step up his efforts; it's not just Congress and the voters who have been misguided. Those close to the president say he understands the seriousness of global warming. But despite the issue's moral gravity, he's been paralyzed by political caution. He leads from the rear on climate change, not from the front.

Work to Make Green History

Forty-five years ago, President Lyndon B. Johnson faced tremendous opposition on civil rights from a Congress dominated by Southern leaders, yet he spent the political capital necessary to answer a great moral calling. Whenever key bills on housing, voting and employment

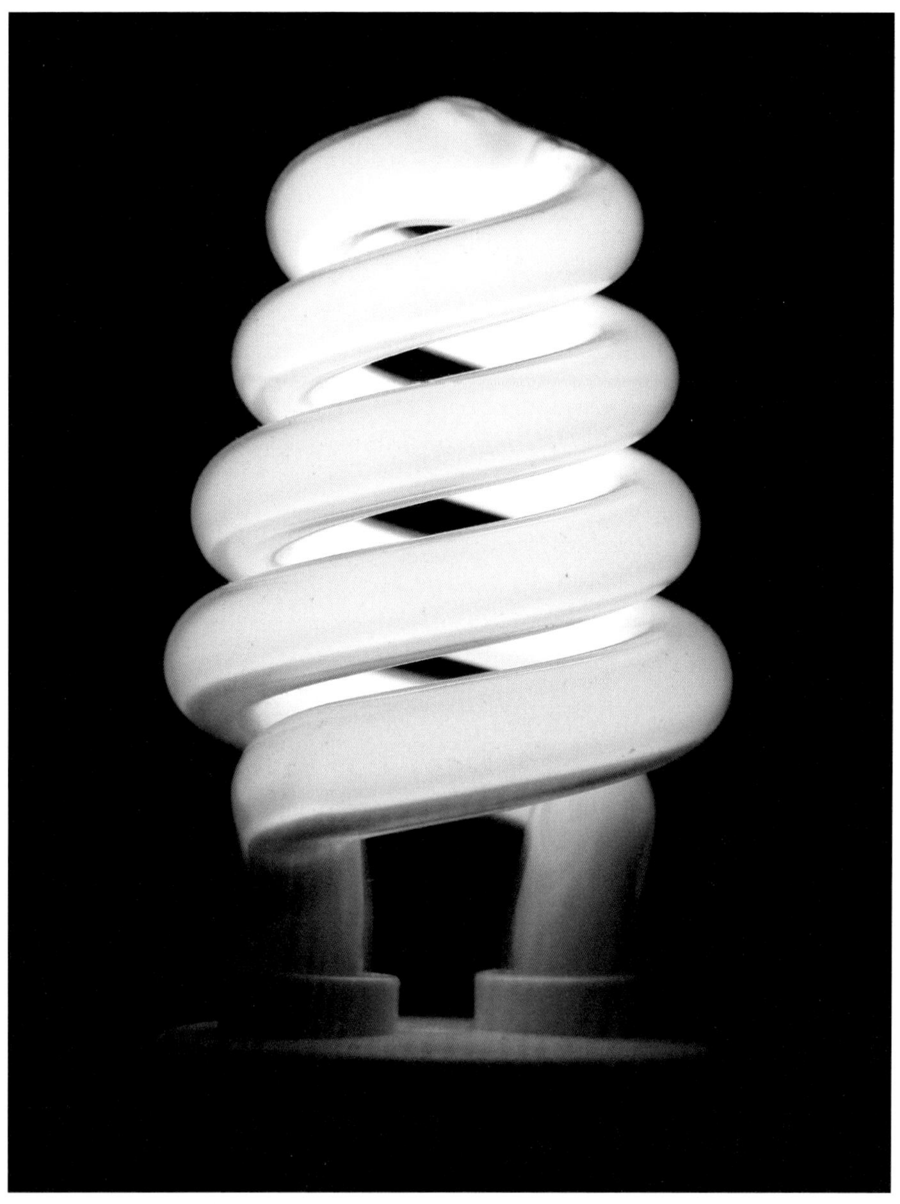

The fluorescent lightbulb is used in only 10 percent of American homes. Americans have been reluctant to embrace the more eco-friendly bulb.

stalled, he gave individual members of Congress the famous "Johnson treatment." He charmed. He pleaded. He threatened. He led, in other words. In person, and from the front.

Does anyone doubt that our charismatic current president has the capacity to turn up the heat? Imagine the back-room power of a full-on "Obama treatment" to defend America's flooding coastlines and burning Western forests. Imagine a two-pronged attack on the fickle, slow-moving Senate: Obama on one side and a tide of tweets and letters from voters like you.

So join me: Put off the attic insulation job till January. Stop searching online for recycled gift wrapping paper and sustainably farmed Christmas trees. Go beyond green fads for a month, and instead help make green history.

EVALUATING THE AUTHOR'S ARGUMENTS:

Mike Tidwell says environmentalists need to embrace the lessons learned from the 1960s civil rights struggle. What similarities do you see between these two movements? What differences? Compare and contrast the civil rights movement with the environmental movement, stating at least three similarities and three differences.

Facts About Environmentalism

Editor's note: These facts can be used in reports to add credibility when making important points or claims.

Environmentalism Around the World

The 2010 Environmental Performance Index (EPI) ranks 163 countries on twenty-five performance indicators that cover both environmental public health and ecosystem vitality.

Out of a total of 100 points, the top ten countries in 2010 were:

1. Iceland (93.5)
2. Switzerland (89.1)
3. Costa Rica (86.4)
4. Sweden (86.0)
5. Norway (81.1)
6. Mauritius (80.6)
7. France (78.2)
8. Austria (78.1)
9. Cuba (78.1)
10. Colombia (76.8)

The bottom ten countries in 2010 were:

154. Benin (39.6)
155. Haiti (39.5)
156. Mali (39.4)
157. Turkmenistan (38.4)
158. Niger (37.6)
159 Togo (36.4)
160 Angola (36.3)
161. Mauritania (33.7)
162. Central African Republic (33.3)
163. Sierra Leone (32.1)

The World Health Organization blames 150,000 deaths per year on the effects of global warming, including extreme weather, drought, heat waves, decreased food production, and increased spread of disease.

According to ThinkQuest, published by Oracle's Education Foundation:

- The human population is expected to nearly triple by the year 2100.
- Rain forests are being cut down at the rate of a hundred acres per minute.

As reported on the website DoSomething.org:

- If current CO_2 emission trends continue, the world's coral reefs could be destroyed by 2050, due to small temperature changes in the oceans.
- The decade 2000–2009 was the hottest decade on record, with eight of the hottest ten years on record occurring since 2000.
- During the twentieth century, the average surface temperature of the world increased by 1.2°F to 1.4°F.
- Polluted drinking water is a problem for about half of the world's population. Each year there are 250 million cases of waterborne diseases, resulting in 5 to 10 million deaths.
- Sea levels have risen between four and eight inches during the last century; experts predict they could rise as much two feet in the next hundred years.
- At least 279 species of plants and animals are migrating north to escape rising temperatures.

Consumption, Pollution, and Waste

According to North Dakota State University's Environmental Advisory Council:

- A single quart of motor oil can contaminate up to 2 million gallons of freshwater.
- A person can walk one mile along an average US highway and see 1,457 pieces of litter.
- Energy saved by recycling one aluminum can will operate a TV set for three hours.

- The Environmental Protection Agency (EPA) reports that, in the United States, 41 percent of all insecticides are used on corn, with 80 percent of these treating a pest that could be controlled simply by rotating crops.
- McDonald's saves 68 million pounds of packaging per year by pumping soft drink syrup directly from the delivery truck into restaurant tanks, instead of shipping syrup in cardboard boxes.

According to ThinkQuest, published by Oracle's Education Foundation:

- If 25 percent of US families used ten fewer plastic bags a month, 2.5 billion bags a year would be saved.
- Every ton of recycled office paper saves 380 gallons of oil.
- By turning down thermostats one degree, fuel consumption is cut by up to 10 percent.
- Attic insulation reduces the amount of energy loss by up to 20 percent.
- Glass produced from recycled glass instead of raw materials reduces air pollution by 20 percent and water pollution by 50 percent.

The website Environment-Green.com reports that Mount Rumpke is the highest point in Ohio at over a thousand feet, but it is entirely made up of trash.

About 1 percent of US landfill space is taken up by disposable diapers, which take five hundred years to decompose, claims Treehugger.com.

Ecoterrorism in the United States

According to the Federal Bureau of Investigation (FBI):

- The Earth Liberation Front (ELF) is a domestic terrorism threat.
- ELF has been responsible for more than twelve hundred criminal acts in the United States at a cost of $100 million.
- An ELF member was convicted of helping destroy a $7 million University of Washington research facility, and others were accused of firebombing a Seattle development of luxury mansions.
- ELF attacks have included a $5 million campaign of Hummer bombings, a $50 million arson attack on a newly built apartment building in San Diego, and the $12 million firebombing of a Vail, Colorado, ski resort.

Job Creation and Environmentalism

The Washington, D.C.–based Institute for Local Self-Reliance calculates that thirty-six jobs are created per ten thousand tons of material recycled compared with six jobs for every ten thousand tons brought to traditional disposal facilities.

According to a study by the Center for American Progress, investing about $150 billion per year in clean-energy sources can generate about 1.7 million new jobs.

Employment in the US wind power–manufacturing sector has grown from 2,500 jobs in 2004 to 18,500 in 2009, according to the United Steelworkers Union (USWU).

The Political Economy Research Institute states that green jobs can help the 78 million people in the United States (roughly 25 percent of the population) who are presently poor and can generally raise living standards for low-income people.

According to the website Blue Green Canada, published by the United Steelworkers and Environmental Defence,

- globally, as of 2010, $531 billion has been allocated to "green stimulus" measures aimed at building the clean energy economy and creating new jobs;
- within the next two decades, green manufacturing in Germany will produce more jobs than that country's auto industry;
- China's total renewable capacity is now 226 gigawatts, dwarfing the 144 gigawatts of its nearest rival, the United States; and
- in 2009, investment in China's clean-energy companies by the financial sector hit US $33.7 billion—a 53 percent increase over 2008—while $32.3 billion was invested in North and South America combined.

American Opinions on Environmental Issues

According to a 2010 *USA Today*/Gallup poll,

- 50 percent of Americans think protection of the environment should be given priority, even at the risk of curbing economic growth;

- 43 percent said economic growth should be given priority, even if the environment suffers to some extent;
- 4 percent said both should have equal priority; and
- 3 percent were unsure.

A 2010 CNN/*Time* magazine poll asked Americans whether they thought current environmental laws and regulations are adequate, should go further, or have gone too far already.

- Twenty-six percent said they were adequate.
- Forty-three percent said they should go further.
- Twenty-nine percent said they have gone too far.
- Two percent had no opinion.

A 2010 poll by ABC News and the *Washington Post* found that

- 71 percent of Americans think the federal government should regulate the release of greenhouse gases from sources like power plants, cars, and factories in an effort to reduce global warming;
- 26 percent think it should not;
- 3 percent are unsure.

A 2011 poll taken jointly by CNN/Opinion Research Corporation found that

- 71 percent of Americans think the federal government should continue to provide funding to the EPA to enforce regulations on greenhouse gases and other environmental issues;
- 28 percent would favor legislation that would prevent the EPA from spending any money to enforce regulations on greenhouse gases and other environmental issues; and
- 1 percent were unsure.

Organizations to Contact

The editors have compiled the following list of organizations concerned with the issues debated in this book. The descriptions are derived from materials provided by the organizations. All have publications or information available for interested readers. The list was compiled on the date of publication of the present volume; the information provided here may change. Be aware that many organizations take several weeks or longer to respond to inquiries, so allow as much time as possible for the receipt of requested materials.

Ayn Rand Center for Individual Rights (ARC)
555 Twelfth St. NW, Ste. 620N, Washington, DC 20002
(202) 454-1997 • fax: (202) 454-1535
website: www.aynrand.org

ARC is the public policy and outreach division of the Ayn Rand Institute. The center's stated mission is to advance individual rights as the moral basis for a fully free, laissez-faire, capitalist society. ARC is named after author-philosopher Ayn Rand (1905–1982), best known for her novels *The Fountainhead* and *Atlas Shrugged* and for her philosophy of objectivism. The site is linked to articles that debate whether environmentalism is necessary, good for the economy, and so forth.

The Cato Institute
1000 Massachusetts Ave. NW, Washington, DC 20001-5403
(202) 842-0200 • fax: (202) 842-3490
website: www.www.cato.org

The Cato Institute is a libertarian research organization that publishes books and studies on various issues, including skepticism about the environmental movement. The stated mission of Cato's studies is to promote policies that leave issues regarding energy consumption, environmental standards, market structure, and technology to the market rather than the government. Its "Energy and Environment" link leads to a bibliography of books, articles, speeches, and events on energy, environmental law and regulation, global warming, natural resources, and pollution.

E2: Environmental Entrepreneurs
Natural Resources Defense Council
111 Sutter St., 20th Fl., San Francisco, CA 94104
(415) 875-6100 • fax: (415) 875-6161
e-mail: cluong@nrdc.org
website: www.e2.org

E2: Environmental Entrepreneurs represents the independent business voice for the environment, speaking for bipartisan business leaders who advocate for good environmental policy while building the economy. Working with the Natural Resources Defense Council (NRDC), E2 takes a reasoned, economically sound approach to environmental issues by relying on fact-based policy expertise. Its website links to clearly written essays, advocacy campaigns, and the E2 newsletter.

Friends of the Earth International (FOE)
1100 Fifteenth St. NW, 11th Fl., Washington, DC 20005
(877) 843-8687 • fax: (202) 783-0444
website: www.foe.org

FOE is the world's largest grassroots environmental group. It is a forty-year-old international network of environmental organizations based in seventy-six countries. FOE campaigns on today's most urgent environmental and social issues, especially in support of developing countries and poor communities. The organization's website includes many resources: photographs, publications, audio links, blogs, animation, and videos. Titles cover subjects such as "Agrofuels," "Climate and Justice Energy," "Food Sovereignty," and "Resisting Mining Oil and Gas."

Greenpeace
702 H St. NW, Ste. 300, Washington, DC 20001
(202) 462-1177 • (800) 722-6995
e-mail: info@wdc.greenpeace.org
website: www.greenpeace.org

Greenpeace is a nongovernemental environmental activism organization that focuses on global environmental issues, such as global warming, overfishing, and commercial whaling. Its website provides links and blogs for many kinds of environmental issues (forests, nuclear energy, sustainable farming, toxins), as well as projects such as PollutersWatch.com and the Greenpeace whistleblowers site. Greenpeace follows global news, politics, and legislation concerning environmental issues, especially the health of oceans and marine life. A multimedia library of photos, slide shows, and videos is also available on the website.

The Heritage Foundation
214 Massachusetts Ave. NE, Washington, DC 20002-4999
(202) 546-4400 • fax: (202) 546-8328
e-mail: info@heritage.org
website: www.heritage.org

The Heritage Foundation is a think tank that researches and promotes conservative policies in many areas, including environmentalism. Its dialogue often takes the stance of government oppression in the name of the environment. The site's environmental subject links lead to commentaries such as "Going Green—but at Whose Expense?" "Twelve Principles to Guide U.S. Energy Policy," and "Renewable Energy Standard Kills Jobs."

International Union for Conservation of Nature (IUCN)
1630 Connecticut Ave. NW, 3rd Fl., Washington, DC 20009
(202) 387-4826 • fax: (202) 387-4823
e-mail: mail@iucn.org
website: www.iucn.org

The IUCN, the world's oldest and largest global environmental network, works to find solutions to the world's most pressing environmental and developmental challenges. It supports scientific research and brings governments, nongovernmental organizations, United Nations agencies, companies, and local communities together to develop and implement laws and policies. The site's resources are on topics such as "Biodiversity," "Climate Change," "Sustainable Energy," and "Green Economy."

Inter-Tribal Environmental Council (ITEC)
208 Allen Rd., Tahlequah, OK 74464
(800) 259-5276 • fax: (918) 458-5499
website: www.itecmembers.org

ITEC aims to protect the health of Native Americans, their natural resources, and their environment as it relates to air, land, and water. ITEC provides technical support, training, and environmental services in a variety of environmental disciplines to forty-two ITEC member tribes in Oklahoma, New Mexico, and Texas. This site features links to the ITEC newsletter, educational events, legislative issues, and various wind energy and clean air websites.

Natural Resources Defense Council (NRDC)
40 W. Twentieth St., New York, NY 10011
(212) 727-2700 • fax: (212) 727-1773
e-mail: nrdcinfo@nrdc.org
website: www.nrdc.org

Founded in 1970, the NRDC actively works to curb global warming, search for clean energy alternatives, defend endangered wildlife and wild places, prevent pollution, and revive the world's oceans by ending overfishing, creating marine protected areas, and improving ocean governance. The site includes the journalism link "OnEarth" and "Smarter Living," advice for going green.

The Nature Conservancy
4245 N. Fairfax Dr., Ste. 100, Arlington, VA 22203-1606
(703) 841-5300
website: www.nature.org

The Nature Conservancy works worldwide to protect ecologically important lands and waters on behalf of people and nature. Its website offers news releases, information about current initiatives, daily nature photos, a search engine that produces articles on oceans and marine conservation, and a link to the *Cool Green Science* blog.

Sierra Club
85 Second St., 2nd Fl., San Francisco, CA 94105
(415) 977-5500 • fax: (415) 977-5799
e-mail: info@sierraclub.org
website: www.sierraclub.org

The Sierra Club is a grassroots environmental organization that works to protect communities, wild places, and the planet itself. Its website features news articles, links to several different blogs, an e-newsletter, and information about both local and international outings.

US Environmental Protection Agency (EPA)
Ariel Rios Bldg.
1200 Pennsylvania Ave. NW, Washington, DC 20460
(202) 272-0167
website: www.epa.gov

The EPA's mission is to protect human health and the environment. Its website features news releases, research topics, information on laws and regulations, a "Science and Technology" section, and a search engine that brings up a wide variety of articles related to the environment, trends, and legislation.

Worldwatch Institute
1776 Massachusetts Ave. NW, Washington, DC 20036-1904
(202) 452-1999 • fax: (202) 296-7365
e-mail: worldwatch@worldwatch.org
website: www.worldwatch.org

Founded in 1974, the Worldwatch Institute is an independent environmental research organization that works to gather and disseminate data on climate change, resource degradation, and population growth. The institute's website features press releases, a variety of blogs, and a list of publications related to the health of the global environment, including its annual *State of the World* report.

World Wildlife Fund for Nature (WWF)
1250 Twenty-Fourth St. NW, Washington, DC 20090-7180
(202) 495-4800
website: www.worldwildlife.org

The WWF is an international nongovernmental organization working on issues concerning the conservation, research, and restoration of the environment. The WWF is the world's largest independent environmental conservation organization, with over 5 million supporters worldwide, working in more than ninety countries and supporting about thirteen hundred global environmental projects. The website includes resources that support WWF's focus on conservation of biodiversity in forest, freshwater, and saltwater ecosystems. The panda remains the WWF's famous symbol of conservation.

For Further Reading

Books

Bevington, Douglas. *The Rebirth of Environmentalism: Grassroots Activism from the Spotted Owl to the Polar Bear.* Washington, DC: Island, 2009. This is the story and examination of the environmental movement, past and present, and especially of three grassroots biodiversity groups.

Chasek, Pamela S., David L. Downie, and Janet Welsh Brown. *Global Environmental Politics: Dilemmas in World Politics.* Boulder, CO: Westview, 2010. A useful overview of international environmental politics, including climate change, environmental challenges of free trade and globalization, and the growing role of the environment in global security.

Dorfman, Josh. *The Lazy Environmentalist on a Budget: Save Money, Save Time, Save the Planet.* New York: Stewart, Tabori & Chang, 2009. Offers innovative and easily implementable suggestions for green living to save money and protect the planet.

Friedman, Thomas L. *Hot, Flat, and Crowded: Why We Need a Green Revolution—and How It Can Renew America.* New York: Farrar, Straus & Giroux, 2008. An optimistic and practical book by a Pulitzer Prize–winning *New York Times* journalist on the need for collaboration and innovation in energy solutions.

Horn, Miriam, and Fred Krupp. *Earth: The Sequel; The Race to Reinvent Energy and Stop Global Warming.* New York: Norton, 2009. Environmental Defense Fund president Krupp and journalist Horn offer business-centered ideas for minimizing climate change by combining the market force of capitalism with high-tech innovation and entrepreneurial inventiveness.

Jones, Van. *The Green Collar Economy: How One Solution Can Fix Our Two Biggest Problems.* New York: HarperOne, 2009. Environmental leader and president of the national organization Green For All, Jones gives ideas for rebuilding infrastructure and creating alternative energy sources, with the double bonus of boosting the economy through higher employment and wages while decreasing dependence on fossil fuels.

Klaus, Václav. *Blue Planet in Green Shackles: What Is Endangered: Climate or Freedom?* Washington, DC: Competitive Enterprise Institute, 2008. In this book, the president of the Czech Republic argues that the environmental movement seeks to restrict human activities. He claims that policies being proposed to address global warming are harmful, especially to poor nations.

Murray, Iain. *The Really Inconvenient Truths.* Washington, DC: Regnery, 2008. Murray, a conservative environmental analyst with a long record of skewering liberals, discusses seven of what he considers to be environmental catastrophes caused by progressives.

Periodicals and Internet Sources

Ball, Tim. "Climate Change Hysteria Falters. Water Is the New Target," *Canada Free Press,* November 1, 2010. www.canadafreepress.com/index.php/article/29408.

Chesser, Paul. "The 12 C's of Climate Alarmism," *American Spectator,* November 23, 2009. http://spectator.org/archives/2009/11/23/the-12-cs-of-climate-alarmism.

Dernoga, Matt. "Environmentalism and Religion: The Climate of Faith," National Bureau of Economic Research, March 1, 2010. http://papers.nber.org/papers/w16241.

Gordon, Richard. "The Case Against Government Intervention in Energy Markets," *Cato Institute Policy Analysis* no. 628, December 1, 2008.

Green, Matthew. "Harnessing the Power of Green Jobs," *East Bay Express* (California Bay Area), May 7, 2008. www.eastbayexpress.com/eastbay/harnessing-the-power-of-green-jobs/Content?oid=1089715.

Greenpeace UK. "What the Green Movement Got Right," November 4, 2010. www.greenpeace.org.uk/blog/climate/what-green-movement-got-right-20101104.

Hagan, Josh. "Save the Planet? Let's Try Saving Ourselves," *Boston Globe,* February 23, 2009. www.boston.com/bostonglobe/editorial_opinion/oped/articles/2009/02/23/save_the_planet_lets_try_saving_ourselves.

Hari, Johann. "The Wrong Kind of Green," *Nation,* March 22, 2010. www.thenation.com/article/wrong-kind-green.

Harris, Tom. "Climate Activists' Exaggerations Will Damage Environmentalism," *Epoch Times,* November 5, 2010. www.theep ochtimes.com/n2/content/view/45462.

Horner, Christopher C. "It's Cold Outside, but Global Warming Industry Still Hard at Work," *Human Events,* December 23, 2009. www.humanevents.com/article.php?id=30028.

Houser, Gary, and Cory Morningstar. "Mainstream Green Groups Cave in on Climate: Dangerously Allow Industry to Set Agenda," CommonDreams.org, April 20, 2010. www.commondreams.org/view/2010/04/20-1.

Kavanaugh, Michael J. "Conflating Environmentalists and Terrorists Is All the Rage," *Grist,* July 8, 2005. www.grist.org/article/kava nagh.

Klaus, Václav. "Green Hysteria Shackles Our Economic Growth," *Guardian* (Manchester, UK), May 1, 2009. www.guardian.co.uk/environment/cif-green/2009/may/01/vacla-klaus-emissions-econ omy.

Kolbert, Elizabeth. "Greening the Ghetto," *New Yorker,* January 12, 2009. www.newyorker.com/reporting/2009/01/12/090112fa_fact_kolbert.

Michaels, Patrick J., and Paul C. Knappenberger. "Scientific Shortcomings in the EPA's Endangerment Finding from Greenhouse Gases," *Cato Journal,* Fall 2009. www.cato.org/pubs/journal/cj29n3/cj29n3-8.pdf.

O'Neill, Brendan. "Al Gore's 'Good Lies,'" *Spiked,* October 15, 2007. www.spiked-online.com/index.php?/site/article/3966.

Parker, Star. "We Need Green Money, Not Green Jobs," *Spero News,* March 1, 2010. www.speroforum.com/a/28150/We-need-green-money-not-green-jobs.

Reisman, George. "Green Jobs?," Mises Daily, April 22, 2009. http://mises.org/daily/3430.

Smith, Wesley J. "Ecocide: A Crime Against Peace?," *Weekly Standard,* May 1, 2010. www.weeklystandard.com/articles/ecocide-crime-against-peace?page=1.

Tapscott, Mark. "Working for Big Green Can Be a Very Enriching Experience," *Washington Examiner,* September 30, 2010. www.washingtonexaminer.com/opinion/columns/special-editorial-reports/Working-for-Big-Green-can-be-a-very-enriching-experience-103963374.html.

Washington Times. "Global Warming Winners," March 3, 2010. www.washingtontimes.com/news/2010/mar/3/global-warmings-biggest-winners.

Will, George F. "Awash in Fossil Fuels," *Washington Post,* November 20, 2009. www.washingtonpost.com/wp-dyn/content/article/2009/11/20/AR2009112002619.

Websites

About My Planet (www.aboutmyplanet.com). A web community devoted to the environment, About My Planet has articles and inviting images. Additional links to services like GrowNews, EcoFriendlyDaily, HybridMile, and GirlSustainable encourage intelligent dialogue and resource sharing among users.

Alternative Energy News (www.alternative-energy-news.info). Considered a leader in environmental news, Alternative Energy News incorporates up-to-date videos and articles about alternative and renewable energies and offers a search engine focusing on the environment.

Cleantech (http://cleantech.com). A website with articles, blogs, and news about green technology, where the Cleantech Group provides market intelligence and insights to companies in the energy efficiency, smart grid, energy storage, water, and green transportation sectors.

DIGG (http://digg.com/news/science). DIGG is an archive that holds thousands of articles on many subjects—including science and environmentalism. It is a great tool to browse for enjoyment or to do some serious research.

Energy Bulletin (http://energybulletin.net). Energy Bulletin serves as a clearinghouse for information regarding sustainability, resource depletion, and the peak in global energy supply. Its online archives contain several thousand articles available to the public. Contributors' politics range across the spectrum.

Energy Planet (www.energyplanet.info). The sister site to Alternative Energy News, Energy Planet is a visual and interactive web directory of information resources about renewable energy technology.

Environmentalism Is Fascism (www.ecofascism.com). Essays, articles, and book reviews meant to "expose both the similarities between environmentalism and fascism and the connections between environmentalism and modern fascistic, or arch-conservative, individuals and groups" can be found on this site.

The Greens (www.meetthegreens.org). This site about looking after the planet was created for kids but is accessible for all ages. The Greens was created by Boston's public television station WGBH and offers games, cartoons, videos, blogs, and downloads.

Insider Online (www.insideronline.org). This website by the conservative think tank the Heritage Foundation houses archives of views, speeches, and policy papers on various topics, including a link to "Natural Resources, Environment & Science."

The Lazy Environmentalist (www.lazyenvironmentalist.com). The website for author and radio and TV personality Josh Dorfman, "the Lazy Environmentalist," this site includes videos, blogs, and links to books and events.

Live Science (www.livescience.com). Easy-to-read, visually attractive, and fact driven, Live Science has been compared with *National Geographic* but with more text to highlight the beautiful photography. Considered a website for both the serious and the armchair environmentalist.

National Geographic (http://environment.nationalgeographic.com/environment). Environmental news, blogs, and travel are offered here with *National Geographic* magazine's high standard of stunning photography and accessible articles.

PESWiki (www.peswiki.co). A community-built resource that focuses on renewable energy solutions, PESWiki is guided by the New Energy Congress, a network of fifty-plus energy professionals dedicated to clean energy technology advancement. Founded by the Pure Energy Systems (PES) Network.

US Environmental Protection Agency (EPA) *Greenversations* Blog (http://blog.epa.gov/blog). EPA environmentalists and scientists write opinion pieces and stories on this blog that can be can commented on by users.

Index

Picture Credits

AP Images/Aaron Favila, 33
AP Images/Ben Margot, 22
AP Images/Carolyn Castor, 109
AP Images/Chip Py, 95
AP Images for Chrystal Light/David Goldman, 85
AP Images/Columbus Dispatch, Courtney Hergesheimer, 74
AP Images/Isaac Brekken, 65
AP Images/Jose Luis Magana, 39
AP Images/Matt York, 100
© Bettmann/Corbis, 76
Scott Carmazine/Photo Researchers, Inc., 10
Marvin Fong/The Plain Dealer/Landov, 57
Gale/Cengage Learning, 17, 27, 35, 44, 52, 62, 67, 81, 93, 102
John Kuntz/The Plain Dealer/Landov, 46
© Look Die Bildagentur Fotografen GmbH/Alamy, 29
© David Noton Photography/Alamy, 13
The Plain Dealer/Landov, 79
Astrid Rieken/The Washington Times/Landov, 48
Zhou Ke/Xinhua/Landov, 61